FROM BROKE TO 7 FIGURES IN 12 MONTHS:

…A 2020 STEP BY STEP GUIDE ON HOW TO CREATE MULTIPLE PASSIVE INCOME STREAMS AND TO FINANCIAL FREEDOM, FROM SCRATCH…

FAB BALE

To my beloved Mother Eliana and
To my beloved Grandmother Gina,
You'll always be deeply missed from the bottom of my heart.
Words cannot express how much.

To my Father Peppo
and to my "Soul Sister" Veronika.

THANK YOU.

About the author: Fab Bale is an investor, serial entrepreneur and business consultant. He is the founder and CEO of several businesses in the US and in Europe. Having started from $0, Fab used the pattern he has detailed in this book to become a highly successful businessman, founding companies across several industries including Hospitality, Real Estate, the Food Industry and Information Technology,.

Contents

1. My story
2. Introduction To Passive Income
3 What Is Passive Income?
3.1 Passive Income V Active Income
3.2 Getting Into The Mindset
3.3 Why Procrastination Is Your Enemy
3.4 Support From Friends, Mentors & Family
3.5 The Biggest Excuses
3.6 Success Examples
3.7 Starting From $0
3.8 What Millionaires Are NOT Doing
4. Personal Money Management
4.1 One Income Stream vs Multiple Income Streams
4.2 How To Accumulate Wealth

4.3 Leverage
4.4 Savings
4.5 Debt
4.6 Know How Much You Can Spend
4.7 Know How Much You Can Save
4.8 Self-Discipline
4.9 Social Media Pressure
4.10 Personal Goals
4.11 Crunching The Numbers
5. Digital Passive Income
5.1 Affiliate Marketing (Passive and Active)
5.2 Pay Per Lead
5.3 Sell Digital Assets
5.4 Sell Physical Products
5.5 Drop Shipping
5.6 Blogging
5.7 Write One Or More Ebooks (Self Publish)
5.8 Book Self-Publishing
5.9 Create An Audiobook
5.10 Build An Online Course
5.11 Money Making Apps
5.12 Buy and sell websites
5.13 Develop An App
6. Physical Passive Income
6.1 Real Estate - Long Term Rental
6.2 Real Estate: Short Term Rental (Airbnb)
6.3 Rent Out Your Spare Room
6.4 Rental Of Assets
6.5 Advertising
6.6 Land Flipping
6.7 Car Parking
7. Passive Income: Lifestyle
7.1 Fitness program
7.2 House Sitting
7.3 Create A Self-Help Series
7.4 Rentable Transport

7.5 Inventory Hire
7.6 Buy A Photo Booth
8. Passive Income: Rewards
8.1 Government Schemes
8.2 Credit Card Rewards
8.3 Cashback Apps
8.4 Couponing
9. Passive Income: Investing
9.1 Buy An Existing Business
9.2 Become A Silent Partner
9.3 Franchising
9.4 Vending Machines
9.5 Coin-Operated Games
9.6 Private Equity Funds
9.7 Crowdfunding
9.8 Peer To Peer Lending
9.9 The Movie Industry
9.10 Cryptocurrency
10. Possible Future Trends
11. Summary
12. Conclusion
13. FAQ
14. Further Reading

1. MY STORY

It was February 11th, 2015. It was a Wednesday afternoon. I can still remember that day because it's impossible to forget the moment you were at the lowest point of your life.

I had been living in Dubai since 2009 when I started up my own consulting firm. I had offices in the UAE but also in Milan, Italy. The time I started my company corresponds with the aftermath of the financial crash, but that was not the reason for the failure of the business. The single only reason was me.

On that February day in 2015, I lost my last client. I tried to find new ones with no avail. My finances were an absolute disaster. I spent the next 6 months living on just €2 a day with no money to pay my rent or anything else. I was 40, broke surviving on milk and bread. No jokes.

Eventually the inevitable happened. I was kicked out of my flat in Dubai. The only solution I had was to call my beloved Fiance

Lota. I had to sink so low as to ask her for a plane ticket to take me to London, where she was living at the time.

Lota and I had been together for almost 13 years. She was 18 and I was 28 when we first met by Lake Como in Italy. I still remember every minute of that day. In June 2014, I asked her to Marry me. We were in Florence and back then things were amazing, we had our whole lives to look forward too.

I must admit that marriage was never my dream. I felt that societal pressure to fall in love and settle down, as many of you can probably relate to. I thought me and Lota would start a family together, but our careers kept us thousands of miles apart.

I didn't like the gloomy weather in London and Lota didn't like Dubai. I know I was wrong, and I should have moved to the UK a long time before then. The plan was always to move to New York or Miami together after getting married. I had spent a lot of time in the US, plus most of my clients were here so it made sense.

Lota paid for my ticket to London, and I left Dubai on July 26th, 2015. I had nowhere else to go and I was completely broke. Lota took care of me and I moved into her flat for a while. It was a beautiful and very spacious apartment, in Mount Street near Berkeley Square Park in Mayfair. It was right across the street from the Porsche cars store. Such a contrast to my own situation. Funny enough the more her career rose, the steepest my fall became.

I fell into a dark spiral and I could not see any way out. Like a black hole sucking me in and no idea about what to do whatsoever. Bad luck has nothing to do with my situation, trust me. My series of negative events made it clear I had to change something. Actually, almost everything.

On December 26th, 2016, Lota and I flew together to our usual Christmas vacation. Her Boss used to gift the top employees a trip to anywhere in the world for the Christmas and New Year's holidays. That year we chose a trip to New York, Miami, San Francisco and San Diego. Those were the last days Lota and I spent together. We broke up at the end of that vacation, which was on January 10th, 2016.

The reason why Lota broke up with me after 13 years, with an engagement ring and a promise to marry was because I was a failure financially, and a failure as a man. No one wants to be with a failed man. There is nothing to blame her for. I had only myself to blame.

I'm telling you my personal story so that you can understand our financial issues can influence our lives... Just like in the human body when we studied anatomy at school, everything is ultimately connected. Things don't just fall apart for no reason, there is always a cause behind it.

After Lota broke up with me I lost everything. Lota asked her Boss' secretary to book me a flight from London to Milan (to my Father's house...), right after flying back from San Diego to London. That was the last time I ever saw or talked to her. She finally dumped me by Whatsapp message (!) one week later, giving me no hope at all to get back together. I had no fight left in me, no money in my bank account. I was completely powerless

- or so I thought.

Fast forward to now, just 5 years later and things are very different. I own several different businesses in Europe and in the USA, mostly in the real estate and restaurant industries. I have several different types of streams of passive income, which have helped me to go from completely broke (financially and personally) in January 2016 to 7 figures in 2017.

I couldn't have done it alone, as it was one of my business partners, Veronika, who totally and literally saved me. She's given me incredible emotional support since we first met in summer 2016, and she still does to this day.

So, you're probably wondering how I did it, and if you too can turn your life around like I did. Follow the next chapters of my Passive Income and Financial Freedom guide, where I will detail the exact steps I followed from January 2016, which brought me to 7 figures only 12 months later.

It's Not About How Hard You Fall...

"Life is 10% what happens to you and 90% how you react to it." - Charles R. Swindoll

We all have a story in life. Things don't go right all of the time, and for some of you out there it might feel like things have never gone right to begin with.

As we move from my personal story into developing yours through better money management, plus introducing multiple passive income streams into your life - it's a good time to reflect on your own struggles that have led to this point.

If I had wallowed in self-pity, and never dusted myself off to become the type of businessman I am today, life would have been very different. I'd probably be heavily in debt, and definitely would never have made it to 7 figures in my bank account!

There is no right time to start learning about money or to change how you deal with your finances in general. The main thing is that you get up and do it in the first place. Stop procrastinating!

So, if my story resonates with you in any way, now is the time to shift the focus from what has happened in the past, to what you are going to make happen for yourself in the present to give yourself a better future.

2. INTRODUCTION TO PASSIVE INCOME

For those who aren't already in the know, earning money doesn't have to come from your job alone. In fact, think of the many millionaires and billionaires out there - did they become successful just from the 9-5 single stream of income? Nope.

Compare it to getting healthy and conducting a healthy lifestyle. If you are serious about it, you're going to be joining the gym, cutting back on fast-food, alcohol and smoking. You might even start taking protein shakes and extra supplements to bulk up and lose weight. Getting financially fit is no different in that if you're actually serious about making it happen - it's going to take more than just putting a few dollars away each month.

The average millionaire has between 4 and 7 income streams. That's not simply going to work each day and feeling satisfied with that singular paycheck at the end of the month. It's finding lots of other streams of income that are simultaneously making them money, even when they are at work.

The goal is to use your active income in a way that will allow you to build passive streams. So instead of relying on active income only, you flip it around so eventually, you will be able to rely on passive streams only. Less working for someone else, more working for you!

Here are a few revenue streams categories that I built up from scratch, that you can follow to go from broke to wealthy, over the course of 12 months:

1. **EARNED INCOME**
2. **PASSIVE INCOME**
3. **INTEREST INCOME**
4. **ROYALTY INCOME**
5. **CAPITAL GAINS**
6. **PROFIT INCOME**
7. **RENTAL INCOME**

Here is a brief summary of each of those revenue streams, before we go into further detail later in the book. This will give you an idea about where I started from, in case you are in a similar situation of having $0 income, or even being in heavy debt.

1/7 EARNED INCOME

Definition: *Receiving money on a regular basis through employment, fully active self-employment or investments.*

We all need a starting point. Whether you already have it, or still in search of it, you need to make sure it exists. The goal of the first income stream is to be able to pay for our basic needs (house, food, clothes). But, there should also be room to save and invest into our next streams of (passive) income too. This means using your savings as money leverage, to create additional income. The more you earn, the more you save to invest, and so on.

If you have a pipe dream of going to rich *just like that* without having ever worked smart or hard in your life - good luck with that! Most likely, if you are reading this book you are exactly in the same position I was in during 2015 (BROKE!). Or close to it. You might even have debt or be unemployed. Or maybe, you simply want a better life. Well, it's time to go out and earn that wealth, starting by getting a job!

You cannot make your money work hard for you if you don't have any to begin with. While it's your end goal to have your passive income streams earn all your money for you, it takes time to build everything else up first so that can actually happen. Similar to how the roof is the last thing to go on a house when you are building it from the ground. Yes - it gives you safety and protection - but it can't happen without solid foundations.

While you might hate your job if you already have one (you can always change it, you know...), the fact remains you need an income to start the process. If you are successful in time you won't need to work because you've mastered your other income streams to take care of your financials for you. Right now however, you need to keep your active stream of income so you have more freedom when it comes to expanding into other passive income streams. You need to be able to see the bigger picture and visualize your final goal.

What happened to me (as I mentioned before), was completely different though, and a lot of you might relate to that as well. I just entered my 40s, and was self-employed as a consultant. My once highly successful job started to be the exact and complete opposite. I needed a change. Something new. I needed to change my professional life completely - to see and do things differently. I tried for a while to look for a regular employed job, but either I was "overqualified", or "too old", or "too risky" to employ.

I'd been searching for about 6 months. In Dubai, in London and in Milan. I emailed thousands of resumes. Do you know how many interviews I had? Only one, and obviously with a negative outcome! In the meantime though, I started to work as an online freelancing consultant, basically switching between my old job, from offline to online, constantly changing the type of services I offered. I analyzed where the highest demand came from, focusing mainly on business planning, personal branding, go to market strategies and social media marketing.

My previous specialization had always been international business development, consulting from my offices in Milan and Dubai. There is one sentence my ex Fiance Lota used to repeat to me. Her boss was (and still is I suppose) a multi-billionaire. "Andrey (her boss, not his real name to keep his identity and privacy protected) never goes into the office. He says that the office limits his business expanding mentality".

Lota also used to tell me, "Fab, you oughta create a business model where you have no offices to go every day." Actually, that sentence, I will never forget in my life. It made me open my eyes, and understand that I had to think outside of the box if I really wanted to change my life and become wealthy. It was like, "Fab.. think outside the box. Don't close yourself away in an office 12 hours a day 6 days a week. The world is all out there.." What a truth oh my God...

So I mostly started to work on Upwork and Fiverr, adapting my previous skills, with amazing results. No more office 12/6. That was how I created a completely new source of active (and partially passive) income. I tell you something, I have always read and studied a lot during my life and career, especially economic and financial topics. Although, I could not capitalize on all my knowledge, as it was focused on one activity only, one profession and one job. Having said that, I have developed so many skills during my career. From computer technology, to photo and video editing, website designing, business planning, social media marketing, and copywriting.

When circumstances or - rather say my silliness - made me

broke, my office job focused on one stream of active income, instead of it being a profitable business. I started to literally cash in on every single possibility of work on Upwork and Fiverr, applying to every single (or almost..) job I found there. This is how I learned to develop my skills even further, that has got me to where I am today.

And, there are so many ways to transform these skills of work into passive income, and we talk about this more throughout the book.

Anyway, in the beginning, when you have to start from scratch, keeping the first stream of income as "active", helps you to maximize profits. This allows you to keep all costs the lowest possible level, using your active contribution to the stream at highest. This in turn helps you to keep costs of automatization at the lowest possible rate.

These days, becoming self-employed is easier than ever before. As I mentioned, I turned to Upwork and Fiverr to start my initial journey. There are so many skills you can earn money from on Upwork (http://www.upwork.com/blog/indcategories) especially.

For example, one of the top-paying skills is Legal entity structuring, with freelancers charging $225 an hour. If you were to put in a 40 hour week, that would generate $36,000 a month, or $432,000 a year minus Upwork fees. Not bad for a job you can do anywhere, even sitting at home in your flip flops! If you want to have a more realistic calculation though, especially if you are not the greatest expert in any field, just divide the above by

50% and you still would get a great return.

In reality, there are hundreds of different skill sets you can put to use on freelance platforms. This includes marketing, design, copywriting, admin, data scraping, coding, legal advice, web design and many more. The main benefit of freelance platforms is you can start for free, so long as you have a computer or internet connection. Upwork even has an app now, so you can respond to clients or bid on new jobs on the go.

For maximum success, you can select '$$$' when browsing jobs, but of course the competition there is tough. Be sure to tailor your proposal to each client, as cookie-cutter responses tend to get overlooked. The more you build your profile, skills and experience, the more you are likely to earn.

Starting at an even more basic level, there are hundreds of jobs you can start for free right now. Here are some examples to give you an idea:

EARNED INCOME: Self Employment

a) Social Media Marketing Consulting or Agency

Businesses know they need to market their business through social media, but many of them don't have the time or skills to do it. Given the average user is spending over 3 hours a day on their smartphone, that's a lot of missed sales and income!

When it comes to creating campaigns on Twitter, Facebook, Instagram (or even just providing customer service through these platforms), that's where your services come in.

For the most part, social media marketing can be done remotely as you can draw up plans/schedule posts either days or weeks in advance. You don't have to physically meet with the client, so you can generate business from anywhere in the world. If you're unsure how to generate stats or reports, you can take a course for free here.
(https://buffer.com/library/marketing-courses)

What you're able to charge will depend on your experience and the client. On People Per Hour, the going rate for a social media manager is between $10 and $130. Let's say you got some experience and were able to put a complete package together for your client, charging $60 an hour. That could generate up to $124,800 a year!

Don't forget add-ons such as SEO blog posts, Google Ads creation and other marketing strategies you can implement to generate even more money from your client. The bottom line is social media marketing is in demand, but is so incredibly easy to start doing for anyone without any big startups costs.

You can even create a social media agency, using other freelancers. This avoids the fixed costs of a traditional agency, creating as much work as possible. This translates into some great earning potential.

b) Business Consultant

If you have any career experience in a particular industry, you can start-up as a consultant, with zero investment/cost.

To start a consulting business from scratch, you first need to know what area you plan on consulting in. To get an idea, start thinking about what you naturally gravitate towards, in terms of your time and interests. While the goal is to make money, it's also about finding where your passion lies. For example, when you are not at work, what books are you reading? What type of YouTube videos are you most watching? These types of details can give a good clue as to what might work for your consultancy business.

You then need to understand where your target customers are experiencing the problems, that you are looking to help solve for them. A great place to start is Facebook groups. Join as many as you can and pick up on the questions people are asking. Look at the common pain points and find a way to solve them.

People value what they pay for, so make sure you set a decent rate for yourself. When you've mastered your craft and collected customer testimonials, this will put you in the frame for a much bigger return from your consultancy business.

The market rate for consultants is between $50-$1,000. The price is so varied because you are free to set exactly what rate you want. It depends on your experience and what you can offer the client.

For example, let's say you become a retail consultant helping small/medium businesses revitalize their retail concepts. You have experience in this field (10 years of your career), and you've educated yourself on the latest strategies. You charge your customers $150 an hour for a thorough consultation, creating a plan that sees them making huge returns when they weren't before.

If it takes 30 hours to help that client from start to finish, that would earn you $4,500. Over a 40 hour work week, that could earn you $312,000 a year (best scenario). Even if you divide that by 50% (safer scenario), you'll still generate a healthy profit.

It's all about hitting on the right opportunity. It's not what makes the most money - rather what you are truly passionate about. After all, you have to be able to stick it out during tough patches, that you aren't going to be inclined to do if you hate the subject matter.

Stick it out, and remember to advertise wherever possible. Aside from Facebook groups, use plenty of hashtags on Instagram and Twitter posts. Create a schedule on a Sunday to generate 2 new posts a day on each platform, directly targeting your demographic. Be strong on SEO, and start your own website building it with Spotify or Squarespace. They are very user-friendly and anyone can build a website with those tools.

c) Blogging

This is a topic we are going to cover in much greater detail throughout the book. However, it's worth mentioning twice because it literally is one of the easiest sources of income you can generate for free, so long as you have a computer and internet connection. In fact, you could literally use your phone to take pictures and write content on the go.

Blogging is essentially writing articles, reviews or how to guides on any topic you can think of. The way income is generated isn't from writing the content alone - it comes from the use of affiliate links and advertising that's displayed on the page.

If you own a business, blogging can massively boost revenue too. That's because most websites are static and don't get updated often enough, which pushes you further down the line on Google. Blogging even once a week shows fresh content on your website, and the use of SEO means people are able to find your website more easily.

So in essence, you can use blogging as a standalone tool to earn money, or use it as a tool to increase visitors to your existing website.

It goes without saying that your blog content must be well written (plagiarized content will not help you on Google and could lead to a lawsuit). If you're not great with words, you can even hire someone on Upwork to write your blog posts for you.

d) Tutoring

Do you have a skill you can teach to others? From music, cooking, chess, math, chemistry, to teaching English to foreign students - your expertise is in demand!

If going it alone, create your own study group where you charge each student $20 an hour (class of 6) or $50 for one-on-one support. That would earn you between $50-$120 an hour, which you could do outside or instead of a regular job. If you clocked 40 hours a week, that would generate between $104,000 and $249,000 a year.

Remember, you can always sell your own courses to generate passive income from your tutoring too. Or, set up a blog with affiliate marketing/advertising. Feature topics from what you teach and link to your private tutoring sessions. That will generate even more income!

These days, you can even tutor people via Skype (much higher potential and productivity). So, all you need to get started is an internet connection, a laptop with a camera/mic and a lesson plan. It's super easy, and a viable way to earn extra cash or create a career from nothing but your existing experience on a topic.

e) Virtual Assistant Work

Businesses need an endless number of tasks completed on any given day. From answering emails, marketing the business, providing customer service or getting on top of admin - it's impossible to do it all alone.

That's where virtual assistant work comes in. All you need to get started is a computer and an internet connection. Don't worry about software either, as your client will either provide this or you can use Google Docs/Google Sheets to create documents, which is completely free.

If your aim is to work in an office but you lack experience, you can use remote VA work to boost your resume. Remember, becoming financially free is all about taking small steps each day. Nobody becomes the CEO overnight!

f) Travel Consultant

If you're well-traveled, why not put your expertise to good use? Become a travel consultant, and you will essentially be paid to organize other people's flights. Even if you are not, you still can learn and research the world's top destinations for your clients.

You can either create your own agency, or submit your resume to FlightFox (https://flightfox.com/jobs). The starting salary is $1,500 a month, rising to $3,000 to $5,000+, once you've learned how the website works.

Let's say you make it to $4,000 a month (you only have to commit at least 20 hours a week!) That would earn you $48,000 a year. Remember, that's not 40 hours a week so fit it around your regular job or another side hustle, and aim to double that income.

We will be featuring this later in the book, but you can also couple your travel consultancy with affiliate marketing. For example, Trip Advisor pays 50% of their commission gained, through their affiliate marketing program. This would equal 5% of the total stay, as Trip Advisor takes 10%. So, say you created your own travel consultancy website and used affiliate marketing, you'd earn

If your travel consultancy business really took off, you could look to partner with airlines and other travel companies to do sponsored trips. There is endless potential from this small idea, which again you can start for free using your existing travel knowledge and grow it from there.

g) Video Editing

Know your way around Final Cut Pro, Adobe Premiere Pro or good old iMovie? The average video editor earns $84,000 a year, so if you have skills in this department and a computer with the software you need, you can essentially start for free.

These days, video marketing is huge. What's more, many YouTubers actually outsource their editing because they lack the time or skill to do it themselves. Even if your skills need a bit of work, there are endless free tutorials you can watch to learn keyboard shortcuts and to develop your editing style.

Many editors also create 'how to' video guides for their YouTube channels or blog. These are then monetized, earning passive income on the side.

h) Translation

Do you speak or write fluently in other languages besides English? If so, why aren't you generating passive or active income from your talents?

Translators can earn between $20 and $50 depending on the language. Whether you translate audio recordings, real time speakers or documents - there is some serious money to be made!

For example, let's say you speak English and Spanish. You work a regular 9-5, but also do 10 hours of translating work a week charging $40. That would generate you $20,800 on top of your regular income a year. All for speaking or writing in another language you've known since birth.

No capital or startup costs required! You can look for translating work through an agency, set up as a freelancer or even have a look on Upwork.

i) Fitness Instructor

The wellness trend is booming as it's now worth over $4.2 trillion worldwide. Fitness is a huge part of this, as people are always looking to shed pounds, tone up or just boost those endorphins.

Fitness instructors teach hundreds of different activities, including yoga, pilates, step, body combat, zumba, dance, spin, kettlebells, gymnastics, cardio, circuit training and so much more.

You could either create classes, private tuition or a mixture of both. For example, say you teach pilates and have 10 students per class, which you charge $10 each per hour. That would earn you a max of $100 an hour. Do it for 6 hours a day which earns $3,000 a week, or $156,000 a year.

Sure, you'd need to factor in studio rental, taxes and insurance - but that still leaves a very tidy profit! Create workout videos which you sell for $300 a series, and generate another $15,600 a year even if you only sell one program a week!

It's super easy to snowball fitness into both active and passive income. We all need to exercise regularly meaning there will always be a demand for it. You could even specialize your routines for office workers who spend all their time sitting down, so they need to stretch their muscles to avoid chronic pain from their job.

f) Start A Planning Business

Good at organizing things? You can literally start a planning business with $0 up front capital. Whether it's project management, party planning, event planning or even wedding planning - all you need is the skills and an internet connection to market yourself to clients.

You'll need to start by narrowing down your niche, and researching what the industry entails. For example, if you want to become a wedding planner you'll need to factor in everything a couple may ask for. This includes finding the right venue, creating a theme, hiring entertainment, getting the right photographer etc. While it doesn't require up front capital to be able to research any of these things - it's going to require some effort.

Whatever niche you end up picking, you can make things easier by creating a spreadsheet of local suppliers/venues etc for your clients to choose from. Eventually you could look to scale the business so you oversee it, with other people running it for you.

While this business is going to be an active effort rather than passive, if you're completely stuck for cash it's something you can start today for free.

g) Food Delivery

The food delivery industry is booming. From Uber Eats to Postmates - the industry as a whole is worth $90 billion in the US alone. If you want a slice of the pie (pardon the pun), then you can get in on it for free by becoming a food delivery driver.

The business model is hugely successful, so you already have a wide plethora of clients. Your start-up costs are $0, though you will need a car (I've even received food deliveries where the guy was on a bicycle, so don't let it stop you if you don't own 4 wheels!)

Let's take Postmates as an example, who give you jobs via the app and allow you to keep 80% of the delivery fee. You can take on jobs 24 hours a day, meaning you can create your own schedule. The platform states many drivers go on to make $25 an hour.

Say you took on a job at Postmates outside of your regular job, delivering food after you get home from work. If you did 3 hours

6 times a week at the $25 rate, you'd earn $450 a week, $1,800 a month or $21,600 a year.

If you're really struggling for cash, imagine what $21,600 could do for your savings or investments? In fact, you could start a business or investment strategy just from your Postmates earnings. The customers are always going to be there, it's simple to use and has no startup costs.

Sure, it's going to require coming home from work tired and then going out again. It's about personal sacrifice to earn enough to do better in life. Plus, the schedule is flexible to you so you can always take a break for a few days, or do extra hours on the weekend to make up for it.

h) Uber/Lyft Driver

You've probably used both Uber and Lyft to get from A to B, but did you know it can also be a great source of passive income?

Why it works is because either ride-sharing platform operates 24/7 making it an easy way to earn money full-time, or around your existing schedule. You could even put your earnings directly into a savings account, or a separate bank account to fund a business idea.

Uber drivers report they average $25 an hour in earnings. This means if you put in 40 hours a week, that would earn you $1,000 a week, $4,000 a month or $52,000 a year. This article has some excellent advice to cut your expenses down (https://www.opinionoutpost.com/en/blog/lyft-or-uber-how-to-make-money#.Xh79l1P7Su5), so that you can take home the maximum amount of money.

Uber drivers get paid for their time and distance covered. Similar to Uber, they can also earn tips. Another nifty feature of Lyft is that drivers can also get bonuses for driving during periods of high demand. The average earnings are fairly comparable with Uber, however some articles have claimed Lyft drivers earn $2 a more per hour on average.

As we will cover further on in the book, you can also make additional money as an Uber or Lyft driver, by selling space on the outside of your car to advertisers. For example, Carvertise will pay you between $300 and $1,200 per campaign. This is easy money and requires no additional effort from yourself.

i) Sell Your Stuff

This one sounds obvious, but in reality, not nearly enough people actually go ahead and do it. Think about how much stuff we actually need in life, versus what we have sitting around our apartment for years without so much as even looking at it.

If you haven't come across minimalism before, you should definitely check this out. Essentially, people who live minimalist lifestyles don't go around collecting useless possessions or junk to fill their homes with. They live a simplistic lifestyle.

To some this is going to sound really dull, but actually in financial terms it makes perfect sense. Say you go out and spend $3,000 over the course of a year on pointless decorations, rugs, ornaments etc - that literally could have started you a business instead.

The point is, you don't need anything other than the basics to eat, sleep and live. So, it's time to get on Gumtree/Craigslist etc and get rid of what you don't need. From clothes, furniture, household tools, jewelry etc - anything you don't use or have no specific need for is cash waiting to be in your bank account.

1) Computer Trainer

Know your way around a PC? There are millions out there who don't (how many times have your parents called, asking how to print or attach a file!)

With knowledge comes power, but also the potential to generate income off the back of it. You could start this business with $0, simply by helping people in their home how to learn what they don't understand.

Charge $50 an hour, or sell a course of 6 for $250. Market yourself with flyers (for those who can't even work out how to create an account!), in local libraries and similar locations. Aim to get 10 clients a week, which will give you $500, or $26,000 a year. If you can scale the business to a full-time 40 hour week job, that would earn you $104,000 a year!

At this point you could franchise your business model (more about this later in the book!), and scale it to a nationwide business. Don't forget to create videos and blog posts to generate passive income alongside this.

m) Home Repairs

If you're handy with a screwdriver or know how to remove wallpaper - put your skills to good use by starting a home repair business.

While you may need to already own certain tools for this business, it's an idea you can once again start for free. All you need are some basic tools (which most people have around the house anyway), some simple marketing and the will to take on other jobs people don't have the time or strength to do.

For example, here are some of the services you could provide: Shelf fixing, floor sanding, wallpaper/paint stripping, painting, floorboard fixing, gutter cleaning, furniture assembly/deconstruction, tile removal, fence building, basic demolition (such as outdoor buildings/furniture) or artwork hanging.

Set your rate at $30-$60 an hour depending on the job and how experienced you are. Say you charged $40 an hour for your services, over a week that would earn you $800 (if you did just 4 hours a day, 5 days a week), in a month it would be $3,200 or $38,400 a year. Work harder and do 8 hours a day, and that could yield up to $76,800.

Even if you had to buy some new tools/clothing etc for the job, if you kept a steady book of clients it would be a drop in the ocean compared to what you can earn. There is always going to be a need for this business, because there are things that constantly need fixing in a home, and people don't have the time, knowledge or skill to do it.

n) Dog Walking

Another simple idea you can start with $0 in the bank. There are just under 90,000,000 dogs in the USA. The thing about dogs is that they need regular walks and feeding.

Dog walkers charge anywhere from $15-$20 per short 20-minute walk, and up to $30-$45 per day. If you have the facility to create a 'doggy daycare', you could create even more income from this, especially as owners don't like to leave their dogs alone at home all day.

Let's say you average $15 per walk, where you walk 4 neighborhood dogs at once for 30 minutes. You then call at the next street to pick up another 4 dogs. Take a 30 minute break, and to go from one place to another. That would earn you $60 an hour, $240 a day or $72,000 a year, if you worked 4 hours a day. Say some owners were fussy and only wanted their dog walking at once? Fine, but add a surcharge to cover the difference.

It really is that easy to start from scratch and generate a huge profit, just by applying a bit of logic. Like many other ideas, you could advertise for free on facebook, word of mouth by talking to owners in the area, or create your own flyers for a very small fee.

To some, dog walking seems like an idea that would never take off. In reality, people all over the country are pulling in some serious cash from it. In fact, once you start to generate a high level of income, you could create that doggy daycare center we mentioned. Or, invest in a dog grooming business and combine your dog walking services with it.

o) Senior Services

By 2060, it's estimated there will be 98 million people in the US who are over 65. Getting older means people are less able to do every tasks such as buy groceries or run errands. Many older people also feel lonely as a result.

There is definitely a market for providing services to the elderly, and the best part is you can start for free. For example, you could charge $30 to do a grocery store run, or $10 to pick up a prescription. You could even consult with the person or their family what tasks they need doing, and have them as a regular client where you help them twice a week.

Although helping others is more inclined towards caring and patient people, it's not only worthwhile but it's a business you can start entirely for free. If you own a vehicle, you could even transport them to appointments or similar errands, again each time charging a pre-agreed fee.

You could even draw up a contract in advance and have the person tick off the services they need that week (try and list 20 for maximum revenue potential). Word of mouth is key with this business idea, so offer incentives if they recommend you to others.

p) Start A Cleaning Business

Everyone needs a clean home or office, the trouble is we don't always have time to do it ourselves. There are entrepreneurs who have created multi-million dollar businesses from recognizing this fact, and creating a cleaning company in response.

It's so simple to start, especially if you already have the tools such as a vacuum and cleaning products. For example, say you charge $20 an hour to clean for your clients. If you were to create a marketing strategy on Facebook (again, for free!) to boost trade at maximum capacity, you could earn up to $42,000 a year. If you don't fancy doing the cleaning yourself, why not set up an agency instead, where you take a commission on behalf of your workers?

If you're still skeptical, it's definitely worth checking out the endless articles and videos where people have started their cleaning business from scratch with no prior experience, yet have gone on to generate 7 figures from it. It's simple, requires zero capital to land your first clients and you can even start today.

q) Garden Maintenance

If you're able to mow a lawn, trim some hedges or even clear some leaves away in the autumn - you can easily turn this into a lucrative business. Similar to cleaning, it's yet another job people don't have the time to do. For others (elderly neighbors for example) they might not have the strength to maintain their lawns or garden. In fact, check out the story of Australia's youngest millionaires (Jack, https://www.youtube.com/watch?v=1YCGM7FiCGg&t=939s), who started by doing just that! Seize the opportunity to make a profit!

While you could knock on doors around your neighborhood, the goal with this one is to get regular clients you go to either once a week or once a month. It's even something you can do on weekends or after you finish work. If you don't have a regular job, this could bridge the gap.
You might think "Hey this is really old school stuff. My Grandfather used to do some gardening work for the neighbors but he never reached 7 figures!". You know what the difference is today? The possibility to leverage any type of job using the internet and social media. Ads have a much much lower cost today than ever before, and you can easily scale any type of business this way. It's also easier to find clients, and let other people work for you, while you only master the online advertising and sales, coordinate the team and enjoy the profits.

EARNED INCOME - Employment

We've focused on income streams you can start for free (or very little). Now it's time to move onto regular income through formal employment. You can either look to just rely on your regular job as your main income source, or combine it with side hustles to supercharge your monthly salary.

The goal is not to look at getting a job as the only way of getting money. Rather, to make sure you have a (high) source of steady income you can then save and invest with over time. The good news is that by following my advice throughout this book, your regular job will not be your regular life for too much longer. It is however, something you need to fix in the meantime if you haven't already.

There is no such thing as becoming a millionaire without getting a job, unless of course you win the lottery. That's why it's the first and foremost primary income stream which you'll need to secure to move onto other income streams.

The primary income source for most millionaires is their regular job. Investopedia (https://www.investopedia.com/personal-finance/top-highest-paying-jobs) have listed the following at the top-paying jobs in the US:

1. Anesthesiologists - $267,020
2. Surgeons - $260,020
3. Oral and Maxillofacial Surgeons - $242,370
4. Obstetricians-Gynecologists - $238,320
5. Orthodontists - $229,380
6. Psychiatrists - $220,380
7. Physicians - $203,880
8. Family and General Practice Physicians - $211,780
9. Internists, General - $196,490
10. Prosthodontists - $191,400
11. Chief Executives - $200,140
12. Pediatricians, General - $183,240
13. Dentists - $175,840
14. Nurse Anesthetists - $174,790
15. Pilots and Flight Engineers - $169,560

16. Petroleum Engineers - $156,370
17. Information Systems Managers - $152,860
18. Podiatrists - $148,220
19. Architecture and Engineer Managers - $148,970
20. Marketing Managers - $147,240
21. Financial Managers - $146,830
22. Attorneys - $144,230
23. Sales Managers - $140,320
24. Natural Sciences Managers - $139,680
25. Compensation and Benefits Managers - $132,860

This list is really useful for seeing where the money is at if you are still deciding on your career, or thinking of making a change. It isn't however definitive. You don't need a degree from medical school to earn a good amount of money from your job. In fact, you don't necessarily need a high paying job to become financially independent.

It once again falls down to the mindset of "I'm tired of being broke". Because only if that statement is true to the very core of who you are, will you have the perseverance to actually go out and do something about it.

Let's look at it from another angle. Say you aren't qualified to work in any of the above industries and have no means or desire to work in them. Why not go after a job at the top-paying companies instead?

According to CNBC's financial segment "Make It" (https://www.cnbc.com/2019/09/18/the-10-highest-paying-companies-in-2019-according-to-glassdoor.html), here are the top 10 highest companies to work for, along with their average salary:

1. Palo Alto Networks - $170,929
2. Nvidia - $170,068
3. Twitter - $162,852
4. Gilead Sciences - $162,210
5. Google - $161,254
6. VMware - $158,063
7. LinkedIn - $157,402
8. Facebook - $152,962
9. Salesforce - $150,379
10. Microsoft - $148,068

For some of you that list might look a little intimidating. The truth is unless you aim high with anything you do in life, you're unlikely to succeed. Aiming for the best possible paid job you can get (even if it does take working up through the company) is a sure way to increase your earning potential.

Though, you should always be prepared for rejection and have a plan B/plan C. We never plan to fail, we fail to plan. Dream big and fail big. But always start from something safe (such as a regular paying job) and work on something bigger like I did. From there, you can start to build your wealth and become a perpetual learning machine. Never forget: The more you learn - the more you earn.

At the time of writing this book, the above companies have a combined total of 22,900 current vacancies. TWENTY TWO THOUSAND AND NINE HUNDRED. Written in capitals for all those who think "they couldn't possibly have a job for me". It's time to change your mindset. Or, you could just let almost 23,000 other folks submit their resume and get hired instead?

Getting a good paying job is essential if it's not your current reality. That might mean leaving the comforts of your small town life behind for bigger things. It's not easy. It takes guts. You will be rejected over and over before you make it. But, you have to make the change to achieve better things.

Plus, if you are living in a small town or in the middle of nowhere, not only are you limited to the number of jobs, you're also limited to the amount of people. It's important to network and climb your way to the top of the ladder, which is impossible without having the right influencers to connect with.

Check out your town's average salary compared with the capital of your state, or even other states. What are people earning compared to you? If your salary is significantly lower especially for the same job then it's time to move on and do better.

The plan is not to commit yourself to a life of working either. Otherwise, what would even be the point of this book? I don't believe in that life and neither should you. It is however a necessary step for now, as you need to accrue wealth in order to build it. The best way to earn money in the first place to do that is with a job.

The idea is to work smarter, not harder (well eventually harder too, but definitely first smarter!). Right now though, the smartest thing to do is to secure a good paying job so you can make the rest happen, through clever money management not to mention passive income streams.

When you think about it, the 9-5 is a financial cage. Sure it's keeping your mortgage paid, but is it allowing you to slowly ditch working altogether? See, passive income is all about things going on in the background that are contributing towards your personal wealth. The more income streams you have, the more you will earn. The more you earn, the more likely it is that you can save, invest and hit those all-important personal goals. Those who really nail passive income can quit working altogether.

But don't rush to tell your boss you quit just yet! Think of passive income is like a game of chess. It takes patience, strategy and knowledge to truly make it work for you. While it's wholly possible to make a living solely off passive income, it needs to be something you gradually build overtime alongside your regular income.

Say you currently earn just $2,000 a month... Does that mean you should give up hope? When you go back to my original story, you will see I was reckless with my spending and my income completely dried up. I had even less than you, and I still made it work. I went from living off bread and milk to running a chain of restaurants in New York, Tenerife, as well as building a worldwide properties portfolio. This is in addition to creating laundry shops, shoes and clothing brands, and even writing a book! No matter where you are on the ladder, each step to climb up it starts with you.

Everything you are learning as you read this book could be

likened to a chess game. It's all about the strategy. Do you want to be the pawn or do you want to be the king? If you want to reach that all-important "Checkmate" where you overthrow your enemy (living the 9-5 just to get by), then it's time to start taking action. Starting with no or little capital, you will progress to reaching 7 figures in 12 months.

Now you know how to fix your primary income source, let's move onto the second in the list of those all-important 7 steps to reaching your financial freedom.

2/7 PASSIVE INCOME

Income that generally requires none or just a little regular input to earn or grow, after an initial larger effort.

Once you've secured your primary income source, it's time to look for ways to plow your earnings into savings and other methods of income. But, you don't have time because you work all the time, right?

Welcome to passive income. The money-making stream that gets to work while you're at work. Throughout this book we will cover passive income in extreme depth so you can fully understand what it is and how to make it work for you.

What you need to know is why it's important. If you really want to build your capital, you can't just rely on one income stream alone. Remember what we said about millionaires having 4-7 income streams?

Passive income covers literally hundreds if not thousands of potential streams of revenue. It doesn't require a constant effort, and can even stem from looking to reduce your current outgoings (known as reverse passive income).

It's something that works in the background, over and over to earn you money. Whether it's renting out a property or even selling digital downloads. Passive income is constant and unlimited.

It's worth noting that there is no such thing as 100% passive income. Everything you do to earn money will require *at least some* effort to get it off the ground. An example is a blog that earns money through affiliate marketing. Sure, once it's posted it can continually earn you money indefinitely with no further effort required, but you'll still need to write, post and add affiliate links in the first place.

Another point is that passive income is not a "get rich quick" scheme. While you absolutely can become very wealthy through passive income streams (some of our upcoming examples make over $40,000,000 a month!) - it's by no means an overnight thing. Like anything else you do in life, passive income takes time and patience. It's about learning to manage the money you have first and slowing building it through additional revenue streams. Although, it is still possible to do it in 12 months as my experience and this book will show.

The beauty of passive income lies in the fact that it's not simply a case of taking on 3 jobs. Passive income works in the background of your existing primary income source. It can be generated by absolutely anybody, even on a $0 budget.

By reading this book to fully understand passive income, you will learn the essential skills and knowledge needed to create your own. The aim is that within 12 months if managed successfully, you will reach those all-important 7 figures.

3/7 INTEREST INCOME

Money given as a reward for saving or investing from financial institutions

There are so many ways you can earn interest on your existing financial assets, or by creating new ones. The most common form of interest is through savings and investments.

The trouble is that most of us don't save (only 31% of Americans have above $1,000 saved). If we do, we don't go for the best deals when it comes to interest rates or other financial perks the bank may offer. It's simply not enough to have money in your account which you don't touch, because even *"saved"* money should be working hard for you.

Later on we will discuss this further so you understand how to make the switch. Essentially, if you've been banking with the same institution your whole life, only have 1 bank account and don't save... you're gonna want to change that!

In fact, if I were to ask you right this second what your interest rate was, or even what type of bank or savings account you had - could you tell me? If you don't know the answer, how do you know you're getting anywhere near the best deal?

If you are looking to add interest income as a source of passive income, it's going to be impossible if you don't secure a great rate. So, it's time to start comparing your financial institution to others if you haven't already.

Another term to get familiar with is "Certificate of Deposit", also known as "CD Rate". It's similar to a savings account, only the bank will give you a fixed fee for allowing your savings to mature over a set period of time.

For example, say you deposit $5,000 and the CD rate was 2.5%. You'd earn $125 for every year you kept your savings in the account. If there was a minimum 5 years before you're allowed access your savings, that would turn your initial $5,000 into $5,625. The more you save and the better interest rate you secure, the more return for your investment you are going to see.

There will be a very small or no contribution to your 7 figures in 12 months, but it is always good to have a short, middle and long term strategy. Keep some savings from some long term investments separate from the capital coming from the other streams of income. (We will discuss money leverage later).

4/7 ROYALTY INCOME

Money paid by a third party for usage rights to material you have created.

Royalties are money that is earned from the use of something you created. Typically, royalties are commonly associated with the music industry, but with the vast array of digital downloads that covers photography, design, video, templates and so much more - there are so many industries you can tap into to earn royalties.

Starting with music however, and this is what the most loved Christmas songs reportedly earn for their creators **each year** in royalties:

Slade - Merry Xmas Everybody - $641,865
Wham! - Last Christmas - $616,190
The Pogues feat. Kirsty MacColl - Fairytale of New York - $513,482
Wizzard - I Wish It Could Be Christmas Everyday - $231,071

This is before you even get to Elvis, The Beatles or anyone else who has ever had a hit record! When reading articles about the above artists, they are surprised as anyone else that 40+ years after recording a song, it's still taking care of them despite being out of the spotlight for most of that time. It is 100% passive income, and has been for most of their lives!

But, you'd say: "But, those are musical geniuses!" Right? Well, as it happens - music royalties aren't just for chart-topping hits. Think of all the music needed for YouTube videos, corporate presentations and even theme tunes. There are millions of people selling their music online, earning a decent profit from it.

In fact, a lot of new music stars have come from self-producing on YouTube. This includes people such as Shawn Mendes, Tori Kelly, Karmin, James Bay, Charlie Puth, 5 Seconds of Summer, Ed Sheeran and Alessia Cara.

There are also people selling everything from stock photos to illustrations, fonts and videos. In fact, there are endless ways you can generate royalties for yourself to create a source of passive income. You don't need some insane talent for any of the above.

All you need is a great product that people need. Some people even record a door creaking and sell it for $1 a download. How difficult is it to record your door squeaking? Imagine if 1,000 students downloaded it over a lifetime for their college film project… that's $1,000 dollars already. It sounds crazy, but there really is a need for the most basic of sound clips right through to catchy jingles or elaborate illustrations.

Creating royalties is all about rising to that demand, creating a quality product, selling it for the right price and marketing it well.

5/7 CAPITAL GAINS

An increased value of a property or similar assets, resulting in finan-

cial gain.

Capital gains are closely tied with real estate, but isn't the same as selling or renting a property to earn a quick buck. Instead, capital gains looks at the overall rise in value over a period of time to then calculate a return on that investment. Think of it more like a waiting game, rather than an instant return as you will see with typical real estate.

Say you buy a house now for $400,000. In 30 years when you go to sell it, you are given an offer of $2,700,000, due to inflation and any modifications you did just before you went to sell it. You'd then earn $2,300,000 back on your initial investment, minus any taxes and realtor fees.

Or if you want to create a short term scenario, imagine you buy a distressed property for $200,000. You fix it and renovate it for an additional $30k-$50k. If you put the time and effort to do market research and analysis about the area, and are good at interior furnishing/purchasing stuff on a low budget, you might be able to sell it for $330-$350k with just 1 to 3 months of work. Which makes it a potential maximum profit of $100k every 2 months for a total of $600k a year.

You don't have to wait a lifetime to earn a good return on your property either. Most houses will slowly increase with value each year, even without extensive modifications.

The great thing about long term capital gains though is that it's something working in the background. Just by buying a house and paying a mortgage, you are generating a huge lump sum far greater than what you put into it. Some choose to re-mortgage to invest in other properties or businesses. Or, some use it to leave to their children in their will.

Either way, there is more than one way to get into real estate, without it being for a quick turnaround profit. Knowing you have a large sum of money in your house can offer you an emergency security blanket in the case of an unprecedented event. Or, you can just leave it alone to slowly gain value alongside your other passive income streams to eventually cash in one day.

Generally speaking, capital gains is how your own assets (namely property) appreciate in value over time. You will then be able to decide whether you want to access that lump sum and sell your home or re-mortgage to invest in another income stream. The "gain" comes from the difference between the price you paid and the price you sold it for.

Real estate creates a liability, in that you are responsible for paying the deposit, mortgage and any maintenance costs. A way to offset this is by renting it out on a short term basis (Airbnb). If you were to do this on a yearly basis, you could expect to see up to a 20-25% ROI. We will discuss this in further detail later in the book.

Rental or sale of any property you own but not currently living in is important, as it's wasted income potential otherwise.

6/7 PROFIT INCOME

Money earned after operating costs have been deducted.

There are many streams of income that "profit" can fall under when looking at it under a general umbrella term. This includes starting a business and turning a profit on the products or services you provide. Most millionaires will have a variety of passive and active profit income streams.

Whether you are looking at passive or active income streams, the key to making profit is that it must outdo any "losses", for it to truly be a profit. Losses include your initial outlay (buying stock for your business for example), paying overheads, wages, taxes etc. The money you are then left with at the end is your profit.

Staying in profit is the core of running a business, not to mention your own bank account. After all, if more money is going out of your account than is coming in, this will spell big trouble... namely lots of debt that can be very difficult to get out of. The exact same is true for any active or passive income stream you are looking to create: it must generate profit.

The more profit streams you have, the more money you will make. That's the difference between someone with $10 in their account, and someone with $10,000,000. Think about it: the more profitable income streams you have going into your account, the less you will have to work. This means less of the 9-5 and more enjoying your time on the beach, managing your income streams from afar instead of being chained to the office.

7/7 RENTAL INCOME

Businessdirectory.com Definition: *The amount of money collected by a landlord from a tenant or group of tenants for using a particular space.*

According to Housing Wire (https://www.housingwire.com/articles/47847-us-housing-market-value-climbs-to-333-trillion-in-2018), the total value of real estate in the US is worth $33 trillion. We all need a place to live, and so most of us will experience either renting or buying a house. The demand is always going to be there for it, and there is always going to be a profit to be made.

Practically anybody can get into real estate. You can choose to buy the cheapest home in your area, invest a few thousand in it and get a small profit, and then slowly work your way up. Or, you can pay off your mortgage and secure another property which you will then sell on or have someone rent, effectively paying the mortgage for you. Once the house is fully paid off a few years down the line, you can then sell the whole thing again, effectively getting your money back with a profit.

We are going to cover real estate in greater depth throughout this book. It's worth noting that most millionaires dabble in property, because like I mentioned just a few lines up... absolutely anyone can do it. Not only that, but there is some serious money to be made.

Sure, it does take buying the right investment and you do have to know what you're getting yourself into. That being said, real estate has always been and will always be - one of the best passive income streams to add to your list.

In summary: These are 7 potential revenue sources, but they are not exhaustive nor do you have to follow each one exactly to make money.

The goal is to really get you thinking outside of the box to understand different potential passive income streams.

◆ ◆ ◆

The Definitive Guide To Passive Income

Now we've covered the basics of 7 typical revenue types that you will need to become a 7 figures man or woman, it's time to hone in on the most important part of this book: Passive Income.

The reason why this book is focused on passive income, is that all the above streams we described can be or become "a passive way of making money." Well at least all those which do not relate to being directly employed obviously.

We've briefly mentioned passive income a few times before this point, but now it's time to get serious. Do you really want to be turning up to your office for 40+ hours a week, every single week for THE REST OF YOUR LIFE?

No? Well stay tuned, as we tell you everything you need to know about passive income and how it could totally transform your financial future.

3. WHAT IS PASSIVE INCOME

Passive income encompasses a wide range of assets and activities. The idea is that you earn money from what is essentially background tasks. Depending on what it is, passive income typically requires one small initial effort to create something that has the potential to generate income indefinitely.

For example, say you've taken some photographs or videos, and you've sold them to a stock website. Every time someone downloads one of your images you earn a small amount. If your images happen to be really popular this could build to be an excellent earner in the background, especially if you continue to upload multiple photographs. It all stems from that one photograph you uploaded vs making your money from being a photographer which is active income.

One of the oldest and most popular passive income streams is blogging (or vlogging in more modern times), namely because anyone can do it and you can start for free. By writing SEO rich content, people can be led directly to your articles from Google thousands if not millions of times over. Bloggers then earn income from advertising revenue this generates, or through paid product placements. The more times your content is viewed from that one initial effort - the more money you make. Compared to a writer who has to continually write new pieces to earn money from a separate effort each time, which would be the active income equivalent.

Bigger returns are possible on passive income streams such as real estate - renting out yours or even someone else's property. Whether you buy a property and rent it out full-time, or use a site such as Airbnb - every time someone rents out what you already own, you're set to make a profit.

Over time the aim is to grow your passive income so you have to rely less and less on your active income, which for most people is their everyday job.

Furthermore, passive income can be broken down into these 4 categories:

"NO INVESTMENT" PASSIVE INCOME: Create + Share Or Selling Assets

This can include both digital and physical assets. Sharing or selling assets is one of the most popular methods of passive income, and doesn't require huge startup fees.

Physical assets you might rent or sell include property, land, cars or smaller items such as bikes at tourist locations. There are even some companies that allow you to rent your designer clothing or accessories. The list is pretty endless, and if you have some high-value items it can turn in a pretty profit on assets that would otherwise collect dust. You might think: "but I have to own or purchase those assets!" Well not necessarily. You can also manage them for other people who own or have purchased those assets too.

Rent to rent on Airbnb was the first stream of passive income I created, and the second stream beside my online freelancing consulting active income. I started by renting properties in the Canary Islands. The Canary Islands politically belong to Spain, but they are geographically located in front of the coast of Africa, more specifically the Sahara desert. They call Tenerife and Gran Canaria "The European Florida" because the daytime temperature never goes below 21/22 degrees Celsius (equivalent of 70/71F) in the wintertime. This makes Tenerife ideal for short-term rentals for tourists, 365 days a year.

Digital assets cover everything from stock photography and video to releasing your own music. Ebooks and audiobooks are equally popular, as they require just one lot of effort to turn into something that has the potential to be bought many times over. The great thing about digital assets is that you don't require a storeroom to hold your items and there is very little customer service required. The product pretty much sells itself with very little upkeep, apart from marketing.

"NO INVESTMENT" PASSIVE INCOME: "Reverse" Passing Income

Involves cutting your monthly expenses to save money. This in turn becomes a source of income, although it is minute compared to other methods. The focus with reverse passive income is to retain as much as your own money as possible. You can then use that money as leverage later down the line.

For example, say you're monthly incomings total $3,500, but your outgoings are $3,200 which leaves you just $200 to save or for emergencies. By taking the reverse passive income approach, you'd look to get this down as far as you could, say to $2,500 which would leave you $1,000 for savings to invest in additional streams of passive income (money leverage).

There are many ways you can go about reverse passive income. Some of the common strategies include reducing your rent (downsizing or moving to a different neighborhood), reducing payments (such as gym memberships you never use), or just watching your spending more closely.

The less of your monthly incomings you are spending, the more flexibility this gives you to build wealth on the side. The money saved can then be put into a high-yield savings account (more about this later). Alternatively, you can plow it into other businesses or investments. Or the combination of the two. Put it into a savings account until you have the right opportunity to invest in. The goal is to save to invest, rather than just save.

Reverse passive income is not just a great place to start, it's something that everyone should do on a regular basis. After all, if you are spending more than you can afford or if very little is left at the end of the month, you are constantly in a dangerous financial position. That's no way to make it to 7 figures!

"INVESTMENT" PASSIVE INCOME: Buying Cash-flowing Assets

Cash-flowing assets are businesses or ventures that generate a lot of income because people have to pay to use them - such as a store. This method is all about picking the right investment to drum up a healthy return.

There is no shortage of cash-flowing assets you can buy. You could choose to buy a pizza business, or a doughnut shop. You could even buy a laundromat or even an automated car wash. So long as it's a business that has a constant stream of customers that require your business on a daily basis.

The advantage of buying an existing business is that you have some idea of its financial state, meaning less risk compared to starting from scratch. You can ask to see the books, what the running costs are and the type of profit the business is turning over. You may also find a business that has the potential to become a great one. If you have prior entrepreneurial experience, this approach would work well for you.

For example, say you want to buy a juice bar but it's placed in a bad location, or the menu system is too complicated and the business isn't doing great. If you have the time and know-how to buy that business, put it in a better location and iron out any issues, then you can turn it into a healthy cash-flowing asset to add to your portfolio.

Think of it like Real Estate. Sometimes, a property has huge potential it just hasn't been handled well up to now. Construction hasn't taken place and the decor is dated. You go in, open up the living room, re-decorate throughout, fix the problems and sell for a healthy return. Buying cash-flowing assets works the same way, but with a view to keep hold of the business and continue to generate a healthy income.

There are endless websites where you can view businesses for sale, as well as their financial history. One such example here (https://www.businessesforsale.com) is the aptly named Businesses For Sale.

I selected "food businesses for sale" looking at the cheapest to most expensive. I came across Firesale Boba Tea, selling for $25,000. Details of the turnover were not available, but this is something I'd ask the owner for when enquiring.

This is what the owner said in the sale description: *"Fun and exciting opportunity to own your own Boba tea shop and retail store!! Owner must sell to move out of State for a job change. Unique concept of Boba Tea and drinks along with retail space for specialty apparel/accessories. Terrific location with ability to add a drive-thru. Popular and growing Boba tea cafe in a busy shopping center. The Business Owners spent over $100k on the build-out and new tea and refrigeration equipment. You can chase your passion and sell hard-goods* *along with cool drinks in this one of a kind concept. Easy to learn, easy to operate, turn-key business. Enquire today! All reasonable cash offers will be considered. Seller must sell to move out of state!"*

So, I'm not saying you should go ahead and buy this business. But, it does give you an insight, not to mention a few clues about whether this business could work. What looks promising is that a quick search here tells me that Boba Tea Industry is actually going from strength to strength. Plus, the owner mentions the potential for a drive-thru which is excellent for attracting commuters or people on their lunch run.

Doing more research, I found the average Boba Tea portion costs $0.75 to make, yet sells for $3.50. That's $2.75 profit each time. To earn back the cost of the initial $25,000 investment, you'd need to sell just under 9,100 Boba Teas. This of course doesn't cover the cost of staff, taxes or the rebrand you'd probably want to give the place - but you get the idea! If you sold 150 teas a day, you'd earn back that $25,000 in just 60 days.

If you expanded your menu to include many different types of tea and even snacks such as pretzels or cookies, you could reach that figure much quicker. Don't forget meal deals and other marketing promotions to boost profits even more! Once you get the business up and running you could then look at franchising.

That's just one example of buying a cash-flowing asset. There are no set guarantees, and a lot of it comes down to insight and strategy. If a business has a terrible turnover, what could you do differently to change things? If the business is located in the murder capital of that city which is why it doesn't get any customers... things won't change unless you have the money to completely re-root the business.

However, sometimes it just needs someone with a real passion to come in and change tactics a little to make the business work. As with any investment, always do thorough research before shaking hands. Look for that existing idea that just needs some polishing to make it great, rather than total disasters or businesses that are out of reach.

"INVESTMENT" PASSIVE INCOME: Building Cash-Flowing Assets

If your ideal investment doesn't already exist, this method is all about building it. Maybe you want to open a vending machine store or a laundromat, near a college campus to attract students because there aren't adequate facilities. You could even buy a hair salon and rent out chairs to local stylists, through a co-sharing model. Building as opposed to buying cash-flowing assets really is your chance to start with a blank canvas.

The ideas are endless, but it does require a lump sum up front to secure any assets/property etc. It can be much more than buying an existing business, because you may also have to factor in construction, depending on your idea.

Alternatively, you can start a small idea and gradually grow it, such as a small food truck that you then turn into a national chain. It's also going to require time to set up the business in the first place, so it's definitely going to start off as active income rather than completely passive - at least for now!

The aim is to turn your cash-flowing asset into something that runs itself. The formula should be something that can easily be replicated in other locations. Take a pizza business or doughnut shop for example - create a quirky, unique brand that works just as well in Austin as it does in Brooklyn.

Speaking of location, you're going to need to find a good place to put your business, especially if it requires physical retail space as opposed to an online store. If setting up a mobile business, you're going to need to research where your best client base is.

If your business is mobile (such as a food truck), you're going to need to research the best areas to pitch up in. It's about getting the right balance between passing trade without too much competition. For example, in Los Angeles, there is a huge market for food trucks that pull up alongside construction sites (especially in Beverly Hills). There are no similar businesses down these very expensive streets, but lots of hungry workers. So, these food trucks meet the demand and can travel to the best locations each day.

Physical space can either be existing which you buy or rent to hold your business, or you can create a building from scratch. The latter obviously requires more capital, so it again depends on the nature of your business.

If you are looking at buying, renting or creating a space, you need to make sure it's in an area where your business will thrive. If you are looking to open a laundromat but there are already 6 on the block, does your business really have what it takes to steal the competition? Or, would a better idea be to move a few blocks away, where there is a higher demand?

Always do your homework before starting a business! You'll need to decide what you're going to sell/produce or offer, who your target customers are, and what the running costs are likely to be. If in doubt, there are thousands of free videos and podcasts on what you'll need to consider before creating your cash flowing assets. Or, there are low-cost paid ones such as this course from Udemy (https://www.udemy.com/course/running-a-business).

If you've never written a business plan before, you're going to need to get to grips with this too. You need to know all of your costings up front, so that you can really get your idea off the ground. You need to know how much it's going to cost to get your premises, buy any stock or assets and hire employees.

The great thing about cash-flowing assets is that if you strike the idea just right, it can really pay off. It's about spotting that gap in the market or jumping on an idea that has high demand. You need to find what you can build that will really work because of the area, clientele and the existing demand for it.

3.1 Passive Income V Active Income

As explained in the previous section, there are some vast differences between passive income versus active income. The main thing to remember is that your active income requires constant effort. For most of us this entails slogging away at the 9-5 job with no way of escaping. After all, how else will we put food on the table?

Well, that's the old school way of thinking anyway. Introducing passive income: the stuff that earns you money from a one-time effort, or very little upkeep at most. Passive income is about maxing out all of your knowledge and talents, knowledge and efforts so that you have as many income streams as possible. It starts by reading this book! Always remember, the more you learn the more you earn!

In fact, when Elon Musk was asked how he got the knowledge to start Space-X he replied:
"I read books. I was raised by books. Books, and then my parents."

From renting to blogging to producing your own music and selling it online, to investing. There are literally **thousands of different passive income streams**, making it much more accessible than it first seems.

The whole idea of passive income is to slowly free yourself from the reigns of never leaving the office. Never having enough time to spend with your kids. Never having enough vacation time. Never being paid enough for your efforts to top it all off.

Think about those stock images you see of people on laptops on the beach. Imagine if that could actually be your reality? If you master passive income, you aren't chained to a desk. You can work completely remotely. Oh, and your *"work"* will not be your boss treating you like a slave as you've been used to up until now. It will consist of carefully selected passive income streams that practically take care of themselves.

You can even combine your newfound income streams with travel. After all, so long as you have an internet connection and a phone you can work anywhere. The world is becoming a giant remote workplace. You can connect with clients in any country in just a couple of clicks.

Remember when I told you I started to work as an online freelance consultant? Well, I did it from the beach of Tenerife in the Canary Islands. That allowed me to discover another great stream of income, which was renting properties to tourists through Airbnb.

After all, why spend 90 minutes driving to the office when the alternative equals literal freedom?

People resent their job because it's the daily grind of having to spend hours stuck in traffic, just to spend even more hours stuck behind a desk dealing with other people's incompetencies.

But, it gets worse. In the US, workers get on average 10 days of paid holidays a year. That's not even two whole weeks for you to have a break from work. In some parts of Europe, workers receive up to 45 days a year paid leave. That's literally 4.5 times MORE than the USA!

In fact, in the US there is no federal or state statuary minimum paid vacation or public holiday quota. Some employers don't actually offer vacation at all! The average number of paid vacation days is 10 days (after 1 year of service). This steadily increases to 20 days after 20 years of service in one company.

So let's get this straight. You can dedicate the best years of your life to working at a company, and you will be compensated for an extra HALF day per year. Even after two solid decades working at that same company, you still will receive less time off than every other country in Europe, who are entitled to an average of 28 days paid leave, the DAY they start the company.

Once you've sorted your passive income streams and become financially free, you can kiss goodbye to this jail term of the "live to work", "born to die" mantra. The sad thing is that many of these huge companies treat you like a number. Except in rare cases, they don't care about you nor are they aren't interested in helping you become financially free.

Relying on that one main source of active income only (your job) is truly toxic. You can never escape, because you have a mortgage, bills and a family to provide for. Even if you are miserable you must remain working in the job or another, because you need it to survive. But, you don't have to rely on what someone else will pay you for your work while you are in the building. You can create your own income, and multiple streams of it too.

In fact, the more you really look at active income the worse it becomes. It of course is a safety net that allows us to save and build our wealth wisely. But, it's also something we must aim to get away from if we actually want to be able to enjoy our lives instead of being married to our work.

With passive income you're in charge. You decide how much

effort you want to put in, and what you deserve to get out of it. Slowly but surely you reclaim your life and are able to focus on the things that truly matter to you.

Like all momentous changes, it's about starting small and learning the ropes. Passive income rarely allows people to quit their jobs just like that out of the blue, and for many they choose to earn from both a passive and active income.

It makes sense that the more income streams you have, the wealthier you will become. Not only that, but you will have the ability to save more which will give you a financial security net. Having active income alone makes this very difficult, especially if you spend most of your time working at your job.

The beauty of passive income is it can be earning you money 24/7 alongside your active income. YouTubers for example shoot, edit and post their content just one-time. If it is seen by millions of people, that's millions of hits to their Adsense account. If that YouTuber also happens to work a regular day job at an office, they are then earning both passive and active income.

If their YouTube channel becomes incredibly successful, their passive income may overtake their active income. This is just one of the many ways passive income can replace active income, meaning less and less effort is required to earn a living and become wealthy.

3.2 Getting Into The Mindset

Like anything in life, if you want to make a success of it you have to get into the mindset. The same is absolutely true with personal money management and the progression into passive income.

If you've picked up some bad financial habits over the years, then this is going to take time and perseverance to correct. Even if you've dabbled in passive income before, there are always ways you can improve.

The mindset of someone who is financially free, and is supported entirely by passive income, is very different to that of someone who relies solely on active income. Instead of going out to make money, people who live off passive income use specific techniques to ensure only a one-time effort is required. So, how do you make the switch?

It's a gradual process, and it relies on focusing on your goals. That means considering every purchase you make, and carefully looking at your bank statement at regular intervals. It means cutting unnecessary spending, making sure you save wherever possible.

The real freedom is to be able to say NO, rather than being able to say YES. If you can't avoid spending on unnecessary things you are a "money slave". A lot of people will tell you that "making money" is a form of slavery. Don't let them make a fool of you. It is just the other way around. Spending money in an uncontrollable way is the real money slavery.

Then comes thinking about what avenues of passive income

could actually work for you. What are you good at, and what assets do you already have to use? Every stream you are able to set up and maintain means more revenue can be generated.

Read at least one book a week, preferably two or even three. Read and learn as much as you can. Some highly successful people like Tai Lopez, Elon Musk or Warren Buffet read one book a day. Choose titles from some of the most successful entrepreneurs. In addition, you should read books about financial and economic strategy. The more you learn, the better equipped you'll be for building your income streams. Books will give you the knowledge to achieve new conquests, and learn new subjects which will give you the opportunity to start new and additional streams of income. Most of the ideas I had for businesses came from reading books. Become a perpetual learning machine.

Start to brainstorm ideas. You should be constantly looking to challenge yourself. If you can't break into a particular stream, see if there is another way around it. Look at other forms of investment, even if for now you start off with reverse passive income, by cutting some of your existing outgoings.

Meet people. Not any people. Meet the right people, who can be important for your future business. Always remember that "your net worth is your network". Let me recommend you a book about this topic. "Never Eat Alone" by Keith Ferrazzi. Choose at least one mentor and let them guide you with their advice. Or more than one. One who is already today where you want to be tomorrow.

The more determined you are to succeed, the more likely you

will. It requires an active shift in your mindset to move away from what has likely been your everyday life for many years - being on the 9-5 treadmill, living from paycheck to paycheck. That life is not only unsustainable, it's making you miserable. It offers no security or chance to break free in the long run.

Write down in advance on a notebook all the milestones you want to achieve, and all your goals. Write them out 12 times a day. Do it with your pen, not with your laptop or cell phone. Visualize the price in advance. See it yours already and write a plan to follow in order to achieve it. This is the way to tell the Universe what you want and desire.

Never forget to say "Thank you" along the journey. Thank people, thank enemies, thank God if you believe in God or thank the Universe if you don't believe in God. Thank every and each one of them every time the Universe gives you what you have asked and foreseen. These things work. Trust me. Smart work, works. Trust me. Do not simply work harder, but rather work smarter. It has to be a combination of multiple factors.

Ultimately you have to really want it. Think of it like a weight loss journey. At first it seems like an impossible mountain to climb but you know unless you reach that summit, you are going to be limited, not to mention unhappy. After all, you didn't reach the point of buying this book because your regular job is financially satisfying you. You've made the first step and now it's time to complete the rest of the marathon. Stick with it, and financial freedom awaits.

All I ask you is that you give 12 months of sacrifices, for a life of unlimited happiness, financial freedom and prosperity.

3.3 Why Procrastination Is Your Enemy

"Delaying or postponing the completion of important tasks."

One of the biggest threats to this entire process that is literally stopping you from achieving your goals is procrastination. Stupid distractions that cost you your focus, drive and energy to get things done.

Putting things off because they are "difficult" or "boring". Replacing a critical task with a meaningless waste of your time - it's time to stop!

In the digital age, the biggest enabler of procrastination is social media. The average person spends 2 hours and 20 minutes a day on social media. That's 34 DAYS a year. Over a whole month... and that's just the average person! More and more of us are constantly glued to our screens scrolling through pointless notifications all day long, even when we should be working.

Remember what I said before about money slavery? Then learn to say NO. This is the strongest form of Freedom and the real key to productivity. Say NO to waste time in any form. Stay focused on your goal and spend every minute of your day to achieve this. Once again - make 12 months of sacrifices for a lifetime of happiness and freedom.

Sure, social media can help our business by working as a marketing tool that has the potential to reach billions. But let's face it for most of it us, it rules our lives and most of the time in a negative way. All of this time playing pointless personality quizzes to share with friends, or messing with unrealistic filters on Snapchat. Even getting caught up reading endless articles. Or even getting into arguments on Facebook. WHY?

All of this is totally pointless and worse still is destructive behavior. If you are one of the millions of people that "don't have time" to start a business, or a side hustle, or even just sort their life out but have time to waste your life away on Facebook... take a good look in the mirror at where things are going wrong. It's all about priorities, and social media should be bottom of the list.

The problem is it's designed to be addictive, like most things we end up procrastinating on. The more time you spend procrastinating, the less/the slower the progress you make.

Think about it in more serious terms. We only have so long on this planet, nobody knows when their time is going to be up. Imagine getting to the end of your life and regretting how much time you wasted on stupid crap like social media, box sets or watching endless cat videos online instead of getting your life sorted? Nobody wants to reach that point thinking "if only" instead of, "I did it".

There is no other option than to cut procrastination out altogether. As Casey Neistat says, "Do more" - the guy has a point! If you've been working too hard and need a break, go catch up with friends, family or mentors around the dinner table - not through a screen. Meet new people, and grow your network.

Eat well and exercise to maintain your health but also your focus. If you are eating a poor diet full of fried food and sugar it will be impossible for you to focus no matter what you do. Your energy levels will constantly peak and then crash. You will go on to develop a whole range of other health problems.

Now is the time for a complete overhaul so you can concentrate on turning your life around to get financial freedom. Unless you think Bill Gates or Mark Zuckerberg made their billions by looking at cats on the internet all day?

At the very least, if you've become an expert in social media with skills such as photo filters or video editing - you could use those skills in a much more productive way than simply posting your personal life's pictures! Or perhaps you're great with your Instagram page, or an amazing amateur photographer and great at editing pictures? Turn this into profit by running social media for small businesses. It's something you can start for free today!

3.4 Support From Friends, Mentors & Family

The cold hard truth is that when the champagne is flowing, everyone is your best friend. When you're flat broke and struggling, nobody wants to know - except of course those who truly believe in you and love you no matter what.

Starting a business or any financial overhaul is really, really difficult. That's why most people fail before they make it (like my story I told you at the start). It could even be you right now, struggling to make ends meet, worrying about how you are going to pay your bills.

Getting support from your friends and family is either going to give you the boost you need, or be the hardest thing to deal with when they ridicule you for trying. What you have to remember is people hate what they don't understand.

Some of the opposition is actually going to originate from feelings of failure from the person spouting criticism at you. There is also a lot of pressure on men to be the providers, and take care of their family. If you're currently unable to do that it can lead to some really dark struggles.

Whether you have a whole army of people acting as your cheerleaders or whether you are going it alone with little support - always keep your eyes focused on the prize.

You're going to come up against some difficulties but it's all going to be worth it in the end. Nothing worth having comes without a lot of hard work. We are so used to seeing people winning but rarely do we see the journey of how they actually got there.

Nobody wakes up and suddenly becomes an Olympic champion overnight. There are years and years of training that go into those few seconds on the track. Yet all we see is the glory. We don't see the years of getting up at 5am to train. We don't see the pain of broken relationships because of the dedication it takes to be a medal contender. We don't see the painful injuries they get at training. All we see is those few euphoric seconds, at the end of the race.

You need to start by stopping comparing yourself to others. This is yet another reason why social media is so dangerous. We see others living these amazing lives, wishing we had what they have - but it's all a facade. It's tiny filtered snippets of someone's life - move on and stay in the real world. Compare you today's self with your yesterday's self. That's the only good comparison you should make. Be better than yesterday, but not as good as tomorrow.

On this journey to financial freedom, there are going to be people that don't believe in you. People who say you shouldn't spend time working on your business after work you should "chill out and give it a rest". These are the same type of people who wave french fries in your face when you're on a diet.

If there is anyone planting seeds of self-doubt in your mind about your capabilities to work smart and hard and turn things around, now is the time to step aside from them. If that's your inner voice, now's your time to silence it, because with everything I am sharing with you in this book - there is zero room for negativity. You've got this.

❖ ❖ ❖

3.5 The Biggest Excuses

Oxford English Dictionary Definition: *"Seek to lessen the blame attaching to (a fault or offense); try to justify"* / *"A reason put forward to conceal the real reason for an action."*

Excuses and money go hand in hand with financial failure. *"I bought those new shoes because I had a bad day at work"*... *"I'm not interested in real estate because I can't be bothered"*... *"I don't have time to learn how to save."*

It goes on and on and on. Before we go any further, it's time to debunk some of the biggest excuses you have been using up until this point. You have a limited shopping cart to add various passive income streams into. Excuses are these huge giant, heavy items you cannot carry. Put them back on the shelf!

These are some of the most common excuses people use when it comes to building passive income streams, or just taking a look at their spending habits altogether:

"I don't have time"

This is by far the biggest excuse anyone will give about not being able to achieve almost anything in life - including taking financial responsibility.

There are 24 hours in a day, 168 hours in a week and 8,760 hours in a year. You have the exact amount of time on any given day as every other person on the planet. That includes Bill Gates, Jeff Bezos and every other entrepreneur you look up to.

People use a lack of time as an excuse, even though they have the exact same amount of time in any given day as anyone else. When people say they don't have time, it's like when they say they don't have money even though they are in a job and just got paid. You do have both time and money, but what you also have is *the choice of how you spend them both.*

If you were to break down how to spend the last 24 hours and any of it went on gaming, browsing social media, watching Netflix for hours on end, gossiping with co-workers or any other form of procrastination and waste time - this is where you are going majorly wrong. **Most of the most successful people in the world do not watch TV. They read. They learn.**

In fact, pause right now to look at your weekly screen time on your phone (YouTube also has this feature). You are probably going to be shocked when you see how many hours you've wasted just in the last 7 days!

"My favorite things in life don't cost any money. It's really clear that the most precious resource we all have is time." - Steve Jobs

Non-essential uses of your time are throwing your potential down the drain. It's not the case where you have to give up on relaxing for the rest of your life... more if you truly want to be able to relax and enjoy your money later down the line - **you can't have it both ways**.

Entrepreneurs are busy people. Take Kris Kardashian as an example. Whatever you think of the family as a whole, Kris has managed her kids in a way in which her youngest has become an actual billionaire. Do you think any of that would have been possible if she had spent hours doing nothing, watching daytime TV?

Kris, like any entrepreneur, is on a constant schedule. There is always something going on that is going to be making her more money. Even when she's out at a restaurant, she's actually being filmed by her TV show that's making her tens of millions. Her diary is constantly full, she is constantly working or even better she is constantly adding streams and sources of income.

While the goal of becoming financially free is not to spend your whole time working, it can't happen without some real effort. This starts with re-arranging your schedule so it's constantly productive, maximizing your earnings now so you can relax later.

How you use your time is going to be make or break when it comes to sorting your finances. So, stop saying you "don't have time" when **you have the exact same amount as everyone else**, you just *choose* to use it in a non-productive way.

"I can't be bothered"

These are the exact same people who *can be bothered* to whine and complain they aren't rich, or that they have to go to work because it's the only way they can make money.

At this stage, you need to ask yourself what's really important to you in life. If you want to provide a better life for yourself and your family, where you actually get to spend time with them… it's not going to come from working in a soulless 9-5 job for the rest of your life. Clinging from one paycheck to the next.

People who you admire because of their fancy houses and cars are the very people who got off their asses and did something with their time, while you were likely sat procrastinating. In fact, they might have even been the nerds at school everybody teased (Like Bill Gates or Mark Zuckerberg) who were spending their free time building their company up. Sure, it's uncool... until they eventually become billionaires!

The truth is, without being bothered to put real effort in, nothing we want will ever happen to us. Take a relationship for example. Once you stop bothering for each other, you stop making that real effort and then you stop communicating... that's where the cracks happen and ultimately you break up.

When it comes to getting financially savvy and building passive income, it takes that same real effort. Sure, some forms of passive income might require very little more effort to build a nice chunk of income on the side of your day job. But, even if something requires minimal effort, if you can't even be bothered to do it, because you'd rather spend all evening on Facebook or watching meaningless programs on TV, you are just going to get stuck in the same repeating pattern, of being broke and unhappy at where you're at in life.

Now's the time to start getting motivated. If you don't already exercise, this is a great place to start. The more motivation you have to get fit, the better your mindset will be for strengthening every other area of your life. You have to have a get-up and go attitude to make any dream become a reality.

"I don't understand it"

Learning about financial discipline and on how to make money when you're just used to spending it is a big adjustment. But don't be so hard on yourself! By buying this book in the first place, it's already showing real commitment to wanting to change your situation.

Let's go back to basics. That's the best way to solve an issue. Go back to its roots. Reverse engineer it. Everyone has money that goes into their account and then leaves it again. The goal here is to understand how much is going in, and what you are spending that's causing that to happen. It's also about learning how to generate more income sources so you can become financially free.

It's about achieving a healthy balance. It's also about learning how money actually works. After all, there is little point earning a million dollars by following the advice in this book, and then blowing it all in a week on mindless spending. Not unless you want to be stuck in your 9-5 for the rest of your life, heavily in debt?

Throughout this book we will cover how to manage your money, so it takes care of you properly. Whether you're starting from $0 or have $5,000 in savings or even $100,000…you can start from absolutely anywhere, so long as you adopt the right tactics, strategy and planning.

If along the lines there are still things you don't understand, I really encourage you to do further reading and research. There are thousands of resources you can access for free to learn the basics of mathematics and accounting, right through to starting a business as an entrepreneur. Being keen to learn is the difference between understanding and not, because it's *your responsibility* to fill in *your knowledge* gaps. I am also going to write one book for every stream of passive income in the near future, which will be more technical and will explain step by step tricks and hacks on how to make money with drop shipping, Airbnb rent to rent, affiliate marketing, YouTube, Instagram, self-publishing and more.

Always have that thirst for knowledge to improve your skills so your understanding will develop everyday. After all, by simply declaring you "don't understand" with no real plan of action *to understand*, becoming financially free will forever remain a mystery, even if we are spelling it out for you in this book!

"I don't have any money to invest"

This would be a valid concern only if you assume that passive income can only come from large financial investments, which just isn't true as we explained before with my story. I started with zero money on my bank account, no house, no cars, nothing. With heavy debts. Even if you have your heart set on investing in a business or real estate, there are ways of generating this income even when you are starting from scratch. In fact, **you don't need any money** to create your first stream of passive income!

When people say they don't have money to make money, what they are doing *is using their barrier as a barrier.* They have become so disillusioned with their current financial situation that they settle for more of the same, instead of looking for change.

As we will discuss throughout this book, there are endless ways to make passive income. Many of them use your existing skills or assets to generate further income. Over time when you have built up savings, you can then choose to leverage this into other financial schemes such as real estate.

Having "no money" to begin with is simply not an excuse. It's the same as saying you have "no time". We all have time and money, but unlike time, if you don't have enough money you can always find ways to make more! Remember, I start with no money and no job! Not being willing to make more money is linked to "not being bothered" as we have just covered.

If you have money for anything that is not an absolute essential for survival, then you have money to either start a business or invest in passive income streams. You've bought this book which was not money you spent on food, gas, bills or rent. So, it's about owning up and stopping using baseless excuses for your invalid arguments.

Passive income doesn't just equate to dropping $250,000 on a condo to generate some extra income on the side. There are thousands of things you can be doing for free (or for a very little up front investment) that can generate you money alongside your regular income. Actually, I don't recommend buying properties to rent them out.

If you use the same amount of money for a rent to rent business, rather than buy to rent scheme, you can generate between $250k to $350k a year net! No properties you purchase can guarantee you the same ROI. If you want to buy a property, choose distressed ones, renovate it and flip them in the shortest time possible, and repeat.

It ultimately comes down to wanting financial freedom bad enough that you're prepared to put in time and effort to understand it, and actually implement it in your daily life.

Now we've covered the biggest excuses you and your peers are likely to use, it's time to get each of those reasons out of your system for once and all. It's time to get serious about your personal money management, so you can take the first tentative steps to financial freedom.

◆ ◆ ◆

3.6 Success Examples

There are thousands of books, articles, blogs and websites that are filled with passive income success stories. Reading how others achieved financial freedom is a great way to learn, and you should also ask friends, family and co-workers about their passive income streams too. The more knowledge you have, the easier it is to build a set of revenue streams that really work.

Johannes Larsson

25-year-old Johannes Larsson spoke here to Forbes about (https://www.forbes.com/sites/celinnedacosta/2018/01/30/how-this-25-year-old-earns-a-passive-revenue-of-400k-a-year-while-traveling-the-world/#1c7a062d73cb) his passive income, which earns him $400,000 a year, all while traveling the world! It's everyone's dream right? Well, here is how he made it a reality.

He has created a marketing business that now runs solely on passive income, as he explained: *"All of my business income is passive, meaning that if no one on the team worked for a few months, the revenue would be the same."*

How this works is because it runs solely on affiliate marketing, instead of a constant stream of clients that would turn it into an active source of income, rather than passive. Johannes said: *"As long as our website is up and running, our visitors can use it to compare services, and that means we are getting paid."*

The sites his company works with are mostly in the financial sector. The team he employs to run his website, are in charge of looking for new strategies to improve the business model. This leaves Johannes free to enjoy the $400,000 of passive income he personally makes from his website each year, with very little input required.

Pat Flynn

Pat Flynn founded smartpassiveincome.com (https://www.smartpassiveincome.com/about), and is another great example of how passive income can create financial freedom. By 2014, he had already made $3,000,000 on his passive income streams, which he has continued to grow ever since.

It started when Pat created an exam online to help pass an architecture course. In a video uploaded in 2019, Pat states that to this day he still earns $2,000 a month from that course, all through passive income! In addition, he now runs his very successful website as well as a YouTube channel sharing his tips for passive income success.

Pat has since made over $5,000,000 through passive income. He talks about it here in a video (https://www.youtube.com/

watch?v=X_b-bb-3kRs) where he shares his top passive income strategies. Pat said: "Since 2008, I've built several different businesses that have utilized one or more of these business models:

"The FP Model - The freelance to product model. Starting with freelancing and then finding a problem, that can be solved with a product."

"The AA Model - The audience and advertising model. It's one of the most used forms of building passive income online."

"The EP Model - Stands for the expert to product model. The goal is to become expert enough so that other people are going to want to learn more from you."

In essence, Pat wants people to get into the mindset of providing a product that solves a problem. So, in his case, that was to create a website that helped people pass an exam. It did require 18 months of hard work before he turned a profit, but it's a website that over 10 years down the line still brings home a very healthy salary.

3.7 Starting From $0. Follow this path.

There are some of that will be reading this book who are literally starting from scratch. What's important is *not how much you have in the bank at this point in time* - rather the fact *you are bothering to start in the first place*. Too many give up before they've even started, so by reading this book you've already committed to that not being you.

I will break down everything you need to know, but essentially you will be following this pattern:

1. Read/learn - **BECOME A PERPETUAL LEARNING MACHINE. THE MORE YOU LEARN THE MORE YOU EARN**
2. Get your money management and attitude to spending right.
3. Get an initial stream of income (active or passive) with zero investment.
4. Save 25% to invest.
5. Invest to create, or create with zero investment, the 2nd income stream.
6. Save 25% to invest.
7. Invest to create a 3rd income stream.
8. Save 50% to invest.
9. Invest to create the 4th income stream.
10. Save 50% to invest
11. Invest to create the 5th stream
12. Save 50% to invest
13. Invest to create 6th stream
14. Save 50% to invest
15. Invest to create 7th stream
16. Continuing to save 50%, to invest and to grow income.

Those 16 steps seems a lot to digest, but it's actually really simple once you process it. You will be fixing bad financial habits, getting a primary source of income, saving and then growing your money from there.

Once you have a steady stream of active income, you **MUST START TO SAVE 25% TO 50% OF IT**. The money you save can be used as leverage to build further income streams. Also, some income streams you can start for free, so will work alongside your better financial habits and savings, to get you to 7 figures.

It's highly unlikely you will become a multimillionaire by having 1 income stream alone (let's face it, if your job earned you $1,000,000 you wouldn't be starting from $0 or even reading this book most likely!) so creating multiple income streams, while simultaneously saving to invest is key. It also sharply increases the possibility that you will become wealthy.

For example, you've got a job which is your primary income. You've opened a savings account, and you've been able to create some leverage. That leverage can then be used to create other additional income sources such as a blog with affiliate links, renting out property, buying an existing business etc.

However, by diversifying your streams of income, this in turn will increase your financial stability. Plus, this way you'll always be able to capitalize quickly when you need cash for emergencies. You'll also be able to invest in profitable streams or deals that arise.

Starting from $0 is about seeing the journey through bit by bit. You have nothing, right? Well, fix that by getting a primary income. Save your money by adopting better financial habits and opening a high-yield savings account. From there, you will be able to implement the rest of the 15 steps just by saving, investing, earning and repeating the process.

3.8 What Millionaires Are NOT Doing

When you picture a self-made millionaire, you probably see the results of their wealth rather than the journey instead. This might include an image of them on their own private island, or driving expensive cars. You might even look at their real estate online and think: "wow, I wish I lived there!"

Let's cut to reality for a second. Everyone likes to admire the wealth once it's there, but very few are willing to truly put the work in (and change bad habits) to actually get there. They also don't appreciate that becoming wealthy when you are used to being broke, doesn't happen overnight nor is it easy.

Millionaires have not got where they are today by doing any of the following things:

Complaining

While this is not strictly true, you must understand that to complain with no intention of changing anything, is completely pointless. Complaining about an issue and doing everything in your power to change it is the total opposite. The only thing you can complain about is you and your bad attitude/habits. Act quickly to change the situation.

For example, complaining you "never have any money" to go on vacation, so you either don't go or get into debt making your financial situation even worse to do so. Or, spending hours whining about the issue. Neither of these methods will actually change the situation, after all even if you borrow money to go you still have to pay it back.

On the other hand, recognizing your money isn't stretching far enough so doing some reverse passive income or taking on a side hustle outside of work is a way to proactively deal with the situation.

Too many people complain about their situation, when if they just used that effort to actually change what was happening, rather than stating their distaste at it, the situation could be completely reversed.

Watching Daytime TV (or even watching TV in general...)

I personally stopped watching TV a long time ago. I find it unproductive and a waste of time. In fact, getting invested in trash television is one of the worst things you can do when it comes to boosting your prospects. Spending hours consuming dumb, uneducated content just to pass time is a complete waste of your potential.

People with 7 or more figures value their time. If they have "free" time, this is spent reading books, listening to podcasts or researching new ways to build wealth online.

Don't get sucked into watching hours of reality shows or listening to celebrity gossip. None of that is going to build your investment portfolio so you can quit work and live off your passive income.

If you are tired or need a change of scene - go to the gym ("mens sana in corpore sano" as the Latins used to say..), visit a gallery or take a free course to build your skills. Don't spend your time watching TV all day when it will achieve absolutely nothing other than an electricity bill.

It's funny how most people use a lack of time as an excuse for bettering themselves, yet have all the time in the world for Netflix or any other box set/streaming provider. Stop lying to yourself and do better!

Never Leaving Their Comfort Zone

The people who have made it to 7 figures starting from $0 knew that something had to change. This includes the way they looked at money, the people they interacted with as well as the effort they were prepared to put in to make it happen.

It requires leaving your comfort 'spending money' zone to start saving instead. Saving is a lot of effort. Especially when you are starting to build your wealth from scratch and you only have one basic stream of income. But saving gives you the fundamentals to make you really wealthy.

In addition, leaving your comfort zone involves networking with new people every day (Your Networth is your Network....), and not being afraid to approach customers or get sociable. After all, no matter what your active or passive income idea might be, if nobody has heard of it, and you have no viewers/supports etc - how do you expect it to take off?

The art of conversation is really important, as it mastering your digital marketing skills. It's definitely a balance between the two.

If you live in a small town that's deprived, and your idea focuses on the community rather than being online - you're going to struggle. It's about recognizing why your idea hasn't taken off yet, and fixing what needs to be done.

As well as educating yourself, you need to be willing to meet people. Build skills in negotiation to make sure you are getting fairly paid, to slowly build your income up. Any skills which you lack, you need to sharpen them.

Leaving your comfort zone is uncomfortable - as it suggests. But, it's the only way to break free from the cycle you're currently in. Those who take risks and are willing to put themselves forward are usually the same people you admire because they went on to become millionaires off the back of it.

So, it makes sense that by never leaving your comfort zone or being willing to at least try new things, you will remain as you are.

Giving Up

This point is about as obvious as it gets, but when you think about it, giving up is the number one reason people fail in life.

Think about the people who start as an intern of a company, who work hard, progress and eventually become a manager or even a CEO. None of that happened overnight, it was through sheer determination to excel, not to mention constantly demonstrating their worth to the company.

Your financial journey is following the exact same mantra, and is the reason why so many people remain poor.

For example, when you are saving heavily this is tough because it means cutting back on so many things, resisting peer pressure, and accepting a lesser quality of living until you hit your goal. For many, they make it just a week or so before they get paid and blow their money again, or only save a tiny amount.

Millionaires didn't get to where they are today by giving up. They saw the entire journey through and that's what you'll need to do to. Nobody is saying it's fun or easy - it's about having self-discipline to make your goal a reality. If you feel you really want something, don't give up. Success might just be one step ahead, but only if you show real perseverance and resilience.

Quitting is what separates winners from losers, or failures to successful people. Those who've made it to 7 figures have found a way. You saw my story at the beginning, and you've probably seen many millionaires/billionaires who at one stage were made bankrupt. Did they give up just like that? If they did, they wouldn't be millionaires now! Accept this journey will be tough, especially if you are starting from a poor financial decision. However, going through the pain and hard work now is what is going to set you up for the future.

"The best time to plant a tree was 20 years ago. The second best time is now" - Chinese proverb.

4. PERSONAL MONEY MANAGEMENT

Time to start by getting real honest here. The main reason I wound up broke, was I had a really bad attitude towards money and debt in general. I used to have 6 or 7 credit cards and constantly max them out, spending more than I actually earned. I always had the deluded hope that next month I'd earn enough money to pay it all back. I used to have what I call a "negative leverage". I used debt to pay debt... the very opposite of the money leverage type we should create in order to build our wealth.

I'm going to ask you an important question and although you're reading a book and I'm not there to hear your answer, I want you to answer it anyway: What would happen right now, if you lost your job? Would you be able to cover the mortgage or rent, as well as all your other outgoings until you found another job and earned your first paycheck?

The reason I ask you this is not to give you negative thoughts, rather foresee issues before they happen, so you already have a solution in place. It is proven that the most successful people are neither pessimistic or optimistic. They are REALISTIC. They base their decision on statistics and probability. If you only have one stream of income, it is certain you will get into financial difficulties if you lose it. It is certain you probably will be OK if you have 2 streams of Income. It is sure you will be ok if you have 4 or more streams of income. When one or two aren't performing well, the other 4-5-6 will. This is **risk management**. Based on statistics and probability.

People can lose their jobs for all sorts of reasons. If you're self-employed and work dries up, you will have to close your business. Or perhaps you faced a huge legal bill you couldn't pay. Maybe you've been in your job for 30 years and the company suddenly closes. Or, are made redundant or get fired, and struggle to get another job because of bad references.

How will you survive? It's a serious question because the truth is most people are one missed paycheck away from absolute financial disaster. Think about how dumb that is when we take precautions in nearly every other area of our lives, but not our finances. Say you live in a cold climate - you have de-icer for your car, a shovel to get out of deep snow and even a spare tire. Or perhaps you're heading to the beach... you take towels, clean clothes, SPF, water, snacks, shade, toys for the kids. Why aren't we applying this same logic to our finances?

At any given time you should have at least 3-6x your monthly salary in case of emergencies. If that's not possible right now then you need to fix your financial habits so that it is. Even if the extra money comes from a side hustle or even passive income. Or, if you have to take extra shifts (for now). It's going to be impossible to secure yourself against very real threats against your primary income if not.

It's actually estimated that 59% of Americans have less than $1,000 in savings. Those are people who will struggle immensely if they get laid off from work or if they suddenly have huge medical bills. Even car repairs could send them over the edge and into debt. Unless you jump into the other 31%, you'll never break the cycle and never become financially free.

The fundamentals of financial freedom including passive income start with basic money management. It is crucial to understand how to manage your money effectively. If you are living by the 'paycheck to paycheck' mantra or if you are not making ends meet, then this is one of the first areas you need to address.

Balancing the books is what defines a business that works or ultimately doesn't. In this case, your personal bank account is that business. Poor money management will lead to spiraling debts and costs, not to mention a bad credit rating. In this scenario, it's impossible to break free and achieve financial freedom without some serious changes.

Personal money management begins by taking an honest look at exactly how much you are spending and what on. Go ahead and bring up your bank statement so you can do this right now.

At this stage it's important to work out where your money is going, identifying what could be reduced or eliminated altogether. What are you spending money on that is not an absolute essential to your survival? Start by printing out your bank statements, and looking at your outgoings vs the money that is coming in.

It's not about forgoing everything outside of your home and bills, rather learning to prioritize. For example, do you value savings and financial freedom more than vacations or expensive restaurants? It's not a case of you can't have both, rather you can't have either exclusively.

Until you get to grips with personal money management, you'll be unable to progress. You're also likely to spend most of your time worrying about money, instead of enjoying what money can bring you.

Being a personal slave to money is exhausting. The good news there is a better way to live, and it all starts with nailing your personal money management.

If you have poor money habits, the likelihood is this stems from years of similar behavior. You may never have had a good example of money management growing up, to follow on from. If so, the idea of personal money management might seem alien to you.

Similar to starting a weight loss journey or training for a marathon when you've never even been on a treadmill before - it's going to take some radical changes.

Your mindset needs to shift from burning money as quickly as you can to holding onto it wherever possible. You also need to make changes from going to having just enough money to make ends meet to being in a position where you have money left at the end of the month to save.

Although a difficult road lay ahead, the destination is one of glory. Not having to worry about every dollar in your account. Or, not worrying about how you will afford retirement. Whatever your goal may be, it's achievable if you get real about your financial situation.

Personal money management means you are the boss of your future. You can either continue down the path of financial uncertainty or turn off at the next intersection leading you to financial freedom. Always remember that to reach the goal of financial freedom and necessary have to make big efforts at the beginning. We all know it is not easy to save 25-30% of your income when you might earn only $1,500 a month. But it must be done if you want to reach your 7 figures in the shortest time possible. The final goal is wealth and freedom. When you earn $1,000,000 a year it is much easier to save $300K or even $500K. Plus, you still have a lot left to spend for you! And you'll have more and more. Just 12 months of patience and sacrifices...

4.1 One Income Stream vs Multiple Income Streams

Some folks are content with earning money through their job, known as a singular income stream. They coast from month to month, learning to get by on that same old paycheck. Even when they find their salary isn't enough to cover their basic needs, they complain but do nothing about it.

While having a job is always going to be better than having no job (with no passive income stream because you haven't read this entire book yet), it's not enough on its own, and it's still going to continue to limit you.

There are so many aspects that are bad about having just one income stream. For starters, you are **limited** to the exact same limited income every month. Even if your boss gives you a raise, it's unlikely to make you so well off you can quit working in a few months.

From a **RISK** point of view, it's really dangerous. If you lose your job, that's your only income source ripped from under your feet just like that. Compare that with a millionaire with their 7 income streams. Say one of them falls through, so what? They have 6 other income streams to pick up the slack. Plus, they are smart enough to have multiple revenue streams in the first place, so it won't be long until they replace it with another.

If you have one income stream and you get fired, this is even worse news. Who is going to hire you with a bad record? If you get fired for something really serious this could drag on, creating a devastating impact on your finances. It could leave you years without being able to secure another job, unless you have the means to create your own company.

So not only is just relying on one income stream going to limit you, it's not going to offer any security. You're never going to be able to quit working or achieve financial freedom. You will be solely reliant on that one paycheck. If you get fired, or if the company goes under you're screwed.

You wouldn't head into cold weather with just your underwear on. You'd layer up with thermals, a coat, a scarf and gloves. Yet, millions of people across the country are relying on just one paycheck. Why is it we are more sensible when it comes to the weather than we are with our own finances?

It seems like some big secret that millionaires have multiple income streams. In reality, it makes perfect sense. Financial security can not come from one income stream alone. The more successful streams of income you can generate, the more your money will take care of you versus the other way around.

Watching every dollar is exhausting, especially when at the end of it you're only just getting by. You put all this effort in every day at work and for what? Don't just sit and envy millionaires who were smart enough to up their revenue streams - study their strategy and do the same.

Once you understand how wreckless relying on one income stream is (especially to support your family), you'll never go back ever again.

4.2 How To Accumulate Wealth

This brings us nicely onto accumulating wealth. Spoiler alert:

It's not about burning money as fast as you can, or leading a flashy lifestyle.

Accumulating wealth can be broken down into 3 main aspects:

1. Time = money

    This essentially means your time is money, and time spent doing a particular activity should be generating income. If the activity is poorly paid it is not worth your time. So, if your job doesn't pay well and there is no chance of a raise, move right along = **MAXIMIZE YOUR PROFITS.**

2. Do not spend more than 75% of what you earn and limit it as soon as possible to 50%.

    No matter how much you earn, you will never be wealthy, let alone financially free if you immediately spend it. If you go beyond what you earn and are in debt, this is even worse. Do not spend more than 75% of what you earn - save at least 25% to invest.

3. Use your money to grow your money (leverage)

    Once you have money, the trick is not to spend it but to grow more money from it. This comes down to wise investments, for example buying a profitable business or investing in real estate.

We will cover each of these 3 aspects in greater depth throughout this book. The main thing to grasp here is that money won't just appear in your bank account. It's also not going to stay there if you have uncontrollable spending habits.

You need to train your money to work hard for you. That means ridding yourself of impulse behavior that would otherwise derail your savings, not to mention your credit score. It's not going to happen overnight, it's a process that takes real discipline to understand where you have been going wrong up until this point.

◆ ◆ ◆

4.3 Leverage

Definition: *Using capital for an investment in order to generate a profit.*

The goal is to have enough money to use it as leverage to create more money. But, it can feel like a bit of a catch 22 right? To make lots of money, you at least need some in the first place. It might help to think of it more in bitesize chunks. As you begin to manage your money better, you will earn more. You will also save more of it, meaning you have more options to plow it back into other passive income ventures that will then give you an even greater return.

It's about the strategy too. You need to make your money work smart and hard for you, instead of throwing every penny away the first chance you get. For example, say you bought a pair of $200 sneakers. What if you were happy with the ones you already had that probably looked exactly the same?

That $200 could be invested in starting your own vending machine business (you do not necessarily need $5,000 or $10,000 bucks to buy a vending machine. You could rent to rent one…) or create another low-investment passive income strategy. Or, you could have put the $200 in a savings account and kept going until you made it to $2,000 and so on.

Think of it like this: The more you save and invest, the more you earn, the more you'll be able to spend on shoes, cars, bags, holidays etc, aka your ultimate goal to be rich. By saving to invest, you will become wealthy, and you'll be able to sustain your lifestyle to live the life you've always dreamed of.

Leverage isn't about throwing your money away on a get-rich-quick-scheme either. Like any business investment, you still need to do your research and weigh out the pros versus the cons. The point is that leverage gives you way more options than starting from scratch.

Always keep in mind, it's going to take just 12 months of financial sacrifice. It seems too tough right now, but trust me - it will make the rest of your life so much better.

4.4 Savings

When you hear the word 'savings' you are either in one of two camps: It's something you started long ago or the idea sounds really boring.

The fact of the matter is that without savings, you don't have a safety net. Nor do you have the means to afford considered purchases without taking out a loan or winning the lottery. You also have no "Plan B" should you become sick and unable to work, or if your home suddenly needs major work.

When you pay off your monthly expenses, how much are you left with? At this point you need to work out what you can comfortably afford to save.

Say you saved $500 of your salary a month, which is 25% of a $2,000 monthly salary. Repeat the process every month for 2 years and you'll have $12,500 saved. Put it into an account that will give you a 2.5% yearly interest. Eventually, after 3-4 months you'll already have a small amount of capital to invest in other streams of passive incomes, which will quickly start to generate additional income. Soon you'll be able to move from $2,000/month to $8,000, then $16,000 then $32,000 and so on. Remember, this is only from money leverage, the passive stream of income you were able to generate without any investment!

Considering you save $500 a month over 5 years only with no investing. You'll have added roughly $33,000 into your savings account. But if you keep on saving between 25% to 50% of your increased total income by multiple small investments, you will have much more, and you'll be able to purchase properties or other businesses. The list goes on and on, but the moral of the story is that saving is essential and it really does work.

Saving ultimately boils down to the following: The more you earn, the more you'll save, and the more you will have.

Even a seemingly small amount can add up to big bucks over time. Compare interest rates to find the best savings account and you'll earn even more money from your initial investment.

The additional fact is that savings give you options and security. Security doesn't just give you more options, it also means less worry.

When we worry about money, it's normally because we are not making enough and don't have any financial backup. By saving you are already starting to reverse this process.

The key is to adjust your mindset from spending money to saving and ultimately making money instead.

◆ ◆ ◆

4.5 Debt

Most of us will experience debt at some time in our lives, either from college or credit cards. You might even be in debt due to a business loan that you are currently repaying.

Whilst in the past debt may have been unavoidable, you now need to make the transition to being debt-free. Getting out of debt can be a long and complicated process, but unless you walk this road, financial freedom not to mention a good credit score is impossible.

Let's take moving into your first home as an example. It can be really tempting to order items on a credit card or on a pay monthly basis to get yourself set up. The trouble is everything you purchase through these methods will cost a lot more in the long run, and with a whole house to furnish and decorate even a small APR on one single item can soon spiral into huge debts.

If you cannot afford to pay for items, goods or services up front you should always consider an alternative method. In the case of your house, why not buy pieces of furniture one at a time, or second hand? Or you could save in advance and set a budget.

Instantly jumping into any scenario that will lead to debt is reckless and is one of the reasons so many find themselves in crippling financial arrears. As much as it may require personal sacrifice, you should always remember there is no such thing as free money. Whether this is from your overdraft, a credit card or loan.

Always pay off credit card statements in full to avoid getting into debt. If you are currently in debt, then paying it off in full should be your absolute priority. Or even better: **do not use credit cards AT ALL!!**

4.6 Know How Much You Can Spend

Understanding how much you can spend each month once your essential bills have been taken from your bank account, will give you a very clear picture of your financial situation.

It's at this point, that you should start to add everything up using an app or a spreadsheet to see what's left at the end of it. Write this figure down so you know exactly how much you are able to spend.

If you are left with a very small amount, this doesn't give you much flexibility or financial security. It can be confronting to see a low figure, but it's how you realize that change is needed. Whether this means reducing your outgoings or bringing in additional income, you must take action to change your situation for the better.

Once you know how much you are able to spend without going into your overdraft or getting into debt, it's important you stick to it. After all, overspending is never good news.

It's worth noting that just because you know your maximum spending limit each month, that doesn't mean you should make it your mission to hit it. Otherwise, you'll make very little financial progress if you are constantly maxing out your bank account.

Also, say you get a raise at work or you get a side hustle and earn some extra cash on the side. That doesn't mean you can automatically start spending more money. As harsh as it sounds, you really have to say every penny you can. That way, the benefits will last a lot longer than an impulse spree to "treat yourself".

A study was developed by the writer C. Northcote Parkinson many years ago, and it explains why most people retire poor. The study found that no matter how much money people earn, they tend to spend the entire amount and a little bit more besides. Their expenses rise in lockstep with their earnings instinctively.

I'd like to stress that only happens if you let your bad habits run your life, and if you do not apply a correct money management approach and attitude. That is what makes the difference to decide which side of the coin your wealth will fall on. Finally, you have to take personal money management in an extremely serious manner.

4.7 Know How Much You Can Save

It might seem impossible to consider saving your remaining income if you do not have a lot of money left. The truth is that every dollar you save gets you one step closer to a more healthy financial outlook. You need to work out how much you can comfortably save without putting yourself in financial strife.

Start by looking at your monthly income versus your monthly outgoings. How much is left at the end of it? From this, work out how much you can save. To increase this amount, you could always practice reverse passive income. This works by cutting existing spending to generate more income without having to earn any money from other sources.

Let's break your income down like so: 50% goes on basic bills, with 25% for investments or disposable income. This leaves the remaining 25% to go towards savings for unexpected expenses and emergencies. So if you want to maximize the 50-25-25 rule, go with investing 50% of your total income (if you have enough money left after paying basic bills). You will reach your wealth targets fast.

For any kind of saving to work, it's essential to open more than one bank account. After all, if your savings are in your main account, not only are you going to spend them but they won't be earning a decent interest rate. Make your savings account something you never touch unless it is for investments. It's that discipline that is going to allow you to make you financially free in the long run.

It helps to have a goal in mind to encourage your saving habits. Whether it's to secure a deposit on a house or even to save for your kid's college fund. Having an emotional connection to the sacrifice is one of the best ways to spur you on when temptation happens.

Aggressive saving seems really tough at the time. You might even have to forgo vacations, turn down parties and events with friends to save money. People around you are going to criticize you and won't get what you're doing. Throughout it all, you have to keep the end goal in mind because you aren't going to hit 7 figures without saving money first.

4.8 Self-Discipline

Think of all the great athletes, musicians, actors and even entrepreneurs you aspire to. While they might all have different jobs, they all have one thing in common: self-discipline.

It starts by creating a habit. It takes 66 days to create a habit. It is not that much. Habits create the difference between "I can't be bothered to do it", and making it naturally as a part of your daily routine, to become part of your life. It can be threatened by a lack of willpower or laziness. Discipline leads to that habit, which then leads to a change in both attitude and personality. Once you've mastered the basics and gone through the tough journey, that's when you will achieve your goals.

For example, take a gymnast learning how to vault. You're seeing that 10 seconds on TV where they are winning medals to rapturous applause right? What you're not seeing is the 15+ years of 4am starts at the gym, endless training, disappointment and rejection. The persistence to achieve glory that wouldn't quit.

This mantra is exactly what the pillars of financial freedom are based on. The whole notion of: "I know what I want and I'm not going to quit until I get it". That is self-discipline right there! This aligns with what's known as a 'focus oriented' mindset. Have your goal well set into your mind. Have a clear path to achieve it. Write it down. Make a plan. stick to it. Every minute, every hour, every week and so on.

Without self-discipline you can kiss any hope of financial freedom goodbye. It takes adjustment, focus and patience to achieve self-discipline when it comes to managing your finances. Impulse purchases have to become a thing of the past, and you should always be looking for ways to save money. In fact, you should be *constantly looking at every aspect of your financial affairs to see what needs improving.*

Are you the type of person who gets their paycheck and instantly blows it on impulse purchases such as a huge shopping spree? How about booking concert tickets at $150 a pop the day a tour is announced? Perhaps you even eat out because you can't be bothered to cook, even though you know it will cost at least 4 times more money to do so? Does it sound too strict or extreme for you? It's hard to say "NO" I know. To say NO to your passions, and desires. But give yourself 12 months of sacrifices, and you will thank yourself forever.

This is the exact opposite of self-discipline. A lack of self-discipline when it comes to money is arguably why most people struggle with their finances. We all face tough situations when it comes to making ends meet, but none of this is helped by also making poor financial decisions. A lack of self-discipline is right up there with how people overspend and get into debt. Never forget, the real slavery status comes from a bad financial attitude. Being able and capable to say "no" is real freedom.

Our spending patterns can also have a significant link to our emotional state. This can be very disruptive when it comes to self-discipline. For example, you've had a bad day at work so you go ahead and "treat yourself" to a new pair of shoes. Or, you've got a promotion and you "treat yourself" to a new car.

It's not to say you cannot spend any money in response to either of these situations. It's more about recognizing the emotional connection between what you are doing, and how impulse spending can really derail self-discipline.

If you're serious about changing your ways when it comes to money, it all boils down to taking responsibility for your spending habits. Even if you suddenly got a $10,000 raise at work - if you then spent an extra $10,000 in response over the course of the year, you'd actually be no better off than before your raise.

Viewing money as something that instantly needs to be spent is a dangerous pattern. Think about how long it takes to make that same amount of money versus how quickly you spend it. If it's not an essential such as rent, gas money or food - why are you spending money on it?

Understanding your spending decisions is how you break away from being an impulse buyer with no savings and heaps of debt. You need to be able to tell yourself no, and not give in to peer or societal pressure to constantly spend money.

It's not about restricting your spending to the point that you never leave the house except to go to work, and you won't even pay for a haircut. Self-discipline is learning the difference between a good financial decision and a bad one, and having the confidence to stick to it.

Getting a grip on self-discipline is the key to success in many areas of our lives. When applied to your financial situation, it can mean the difference between having disposable income at the end of the month or being in debt.

Overspending in the moment might feel great, but it definitely won't when you see your credit card statement and worry about how you are going to pay it all back. This is what you should think of the next time you go to make an impulse purchase. If you don't need it, why are you buying it?

See, most people value having money but not how to make it. How can you possibly have an abundance of something, when you're not willing to understand how to get it? That's like expecting to have a 6 pack when you've only walked past the gym. It's just not going to happen!

Or, you might have consigned yourself to being broke because that's the environment you were brought in. What you have to remember is that you are not your parents - your financial decisions come solely from you. The past does not have to dictate the future, though it is a steep learning curve to undo bad habits you may have inherited. It's not impossible and it starts today.

Real freedom will come after you are able to say no today, to be able to achieve your goal tomorrow. Let's set this goal right now to educate yourself about money with a goal of reaching 7 figures in 12 months.

◆ ◆ ◆

4.9 Social Media Pressure

Closely connected to personal discipline is how we perceive and respond to social media. More specifically, the pressure to conform to how others are living, or at least how *it would seem* they are, according to their Instagram and Facebook posts.

A report by the British newspaper Metro (https://metro.co.uk/2019/11/21/people-are-getting-in-to-debt-because-of-the-pressure-to-be-perfect-on-instagram-11188264), found that people are getting into serious debt trying to become famous on social media.

We all dream of getting rich. Who wouldn't want to go on endless luxury holidays, have the best cars and travel by private jet? If you read my story at the beginning, you'll know that mindless spending only leads to big trouble.

Spending money you don't have won't make you rich. It comes down to asking yourself why you need thousands of followers. For most people, it's the validation it gives. They see the Kardashians with 100+ million followers and they want the same.

The only problem is the mind of an entrepreneur works differently. Spending money you don't have to try and emulate the success of others is a recipe for disaster. Say you even reached 1 million followers, there is no guarantee you'd earn even a cent back of what you spent to get there. There is also no guarantee a follower count will make you happy or give you validation.

Don't get me wrong here, social media is a place (and most probably today THE place..) where you absolutely can make money. But, everything needs to be done with brains and discipline and again, with a plan. To sum this up - you need good strategies. What's the difference between a strategy and a plan? A plan is a sum of strategies to reach one determined goal.

It all stems back to our relationship with money. Similar to how we spend excessively when we are happy or sad, it's also possible to spend money out of desperation to become something we're not.

If you have any social media accounts, pause to look at the content you are posting as well as following and absorbing. If it's fueling a pattern of unhealthy aspirations and spending habits trying to be the next big thing, you've got to ask yourself why.

Becoming financially free is a dream we all have, but you won't get there by wearing designer clothes when you can't afford your mortgage. Or driving a Ferrari just to take pictures of it on Instagram when you have serious debt you are struggling to pay off.

If anything, becoming financially free is about being smart with your money. That's not to say you can't splash out, but you need to realize that spending cash for the sake of "looking rich" is about as financially incompetent as it gets.

Chasing likes and follows is not a way to earn respect, let alone money. While social media is an excellent marketing tool for your business, it's important not to get swept away trying to become something you're not in the process.

People across the world are getting themselves into debt to fund a lifestyle that's not sustainable, and for what? Don't fall into this trap and treat your bank balance with more respect than that. The goal of this entire book is to make money and keep hold of as much as you can so you can then make more money, not blow it on the latest car just to show off.

An excerpt from the article (https://metro.co.uk/2019/11/21/people-are-getting-in-to-debt-because-of-the-pressure-to-be-perfect-on-instagram-11188264) finishes with some excellent advice. It reads: "'Sure, there's an audience for the latest designer handbag or tropical island escape – but with 500 million daily active users, there's an audience for who you really are, too."

Living within your means is the basis for any financial plan. You are never going to be able to sit on a beach all day if you are $250,000 in debt because you are deeply insecure about what you see on social media, and spend excessively in response. From surgery to cars - stop spending on account of what you're scrolling through.

If you're a millennial reading this you're going to shriek at what I'm about to say, but if you've noticed you are spending excessively due to social media pressure, then it's time to delete or deactivate for a while, until you can truly see the error of your ways.

Unless you want to keep on spending money you don't have?

4.10 Personal Goals

"Dreams without goals remain dreams. Dreams are great. In fact, dreams are necessary in life or no one would ever go anywhere! But a dream without a goal, and without action, has no opportunity to come true. Never confuse movement with progress. Because you can run in place and not get anywhere." - Denzel Washington

Everything comes down to your personal goals. You need to ask yourself: "What do I want to ultimately achieve?" Whether your goal is just within reach or is currently unattainable, it's all about focusing on the end game.

Be aware though that there is little point in having a personal goal that you don't take seriously and aren't prepared to work towards, otherwise it will just become a pipe dream.

There is no such thing as an overnight success. Anyone who tells you that going from financial hardship to financial freedom can be done in the course of a day is lying. That's not to discourage you, rather make you understand that sorting your finances takes real work and commitment. If it didn't we'd all millionaires with very little effort!

So, now is the time to make your personal goals. Write them out and stick them on the refrigerator, on your notice-board, or wherever you can see them. Once you know your goals you can truly start to devise a plan to achieve them.

It can sometimes help to make personal goals in bitesize chunks. For example, "I want to cancel my $100,000 debt in one year". Coming up with an additional $100,000 through better financial management or passive income, is a lot easier to digest or maybe, even just the only way to do it. It will also give you confidence when you do reach that goal, versus setting an impossible target you're unable to reach.

Whatever your goal is right now, it has to be something that will get you out of bed every morning. Something tangible that you are determined to achieve, no matter what. The reason I say that is because unless it means something, you aren't going to be bothered to go out and get it.

That couldn't be truer if you are planning to go from $0 to 7 figures. It's mammoth. One of the biggest changes (if not the biggest change) you will ever go through in your entire life. You have to be 100% passionate and committed in order to reach your goal.

Sure, others around you are going to mock you for it. They

won't get it or understand your transformation (they will be all over you like a rash once you're rich though, watch out for that!) It doesn't matter. All that actually matters is that you are going to set yourself a goal and stop at nothing until you reach it.

◆ ◆ ◆

4.11 Crunching The Numbers

To make $1,000,000 in a year, you'll need to be earning $2,740 a day. When you first read that figure, **it will seem impossible and scary.** What is **actually scary,** is living from paycheck to paycheck working a low-paying job, where you are not appreciated until you retire, it at all! Living that lifestyle will mean you will never ever reach $1,000,000. Add in poor financial habits and you'll probably struggle to make ends meet too.

The only difference between someone who has made $1,000,000 starting from $0 and someone who hasn't is someone who has gone and done it. Note: Complaining about it doesn't count as working towards it.

So let's go back to the tips of the 7 different revenue streams that the average millionaire has. We've already covered your primary income source, which if you follow our advice, hopefully to be far higher than the $56,516 measly US average, but nor necessary. As I showed you with the example before, even a $2,000 monthly could be the start. Or even $0!

Here is the link again (https://www.cnbc.com/2019/09/18/the-10-highest-paying-companies-in-2019-according-to-glassdoor.html) though for the 23,000+ job vacancies for the top-paying companies, that will pay you an average salary of $170,279.

Even if your primary source of income is from self-employment or a business, there is no reason why you can't achieve the same figure or even more! A lot of it is down to strategy and marketing, so this is a good place to start if your yearly take-home figure is significantly less than what you'd like it to be.

"Many people take no care of their money till they come nearly to the end of it, and others do just the same with their time." - Johann Wolfgang von Goethe

If you don't know how to make your business make more money, there are thousands of free resources you can check out. For example, this article from Inc (https://www.inc.com/john-rampton/how-to-be-successful-in-business-and-be-successful-in-life-too.html). Research as much as you can, especially stories from people who have failed but went onto succeed. It is possible with the right attitude.

Mastering the other 7 forms of revenue including passive income is where you can really start to build your money up. Remember, most forms of passive income require very little initial effort and can earn you money while you work.

Watch videos of entrepreneurs on how they overcame their struggles (we are going to give you some links here in this book), read books on business (remember at least one book a week or more!), attend networking events - do whatever you have to do to turn things around. Remember, nothing comes without hard work. The more you put in, the more you will get out

It seems scary to have to hit $2,740 a day because it's not something one stream of revenue will ever allow us to do, except for a very small number of industries (such as law, medicine, etc). But, how about when you break it down into 7 revenue streams? That would mean each stream would need to pull in $391 a day.

When you consider there are thousands of revenue streams in addition to passive income, it's really not that difficult to achieve.

For example:

1 = Primary Active Income (Employment/Self-Employment)
2 = Rental Income
3 = Blogging/Self Publishing
4 = Affiliate Marketing/Digital Marketing
5 = Real Estate Business
6 = Ecommerce/Drop Shipping
7 = Investments

That's not a definite list or guarantee, just an example of how you can break it down. Some streams might earn more or less than others. That's the beauty of it. If one stream isn't bringing in what you'd like, you can either add another, change it or simply get someone to market it better for you.

The more you take a multi-faceted approach to earn money, the more likely it is you will achieve $1,000,000 in just 12 months. Whereas, the more you stay in your current situation just relying on your job to get by, the more likely you will stay as you are.

Once you've taken control of your finances, have eradicated mindless spending and have many streams of income paying into your account each day, that's when you will start to hit that $2,740 a day. It's really not anywhere near as impossible as it seemed when you started reading the top of this section.

Remember, each stream needs to average just $392 a day to make $1,000,000 a year. When you break it down like that, you will see it's way more attainable than you first thought.

It simply comes down to understanding how to manage your money, and taking the steps I share with you to go out and actually make it happen. We will now move onto passive income streams for you to get to grips with, starting with ones you can create online.

5. DIGITAL PASSIVE INCOME

Financial gain generated from the sale of assets online. This includes things such as digital products, visual media, affiliate marketing, online courses etc.

If you are looking to take your first tentative steps into the world of passive income, then looking at digital revenue streams is the perfect place to start. That's because despite the fact that the internet was only invented some 30 years ago, it has an incredible reach. It's estimated that over 4.3 billion people have access to the internet, which is a very large potential audience for anything you are trying to sell.

The internet gives you instant access to every corner of the globe. With the right product not to mention strategy, it's a plethora of untapped potential just waiting for your idea to truly flourish.

The great thing about digital passive income is you can start with **no initial investment.** If you have the means for publishing content (such as a phone or laptop) you're already good to go. In many cases, a passive income built online can even help with your career options too. For example, starting a blog is a great way to earn money from advertising revenue but it's also a great way to demonstrate your portfolio to publishers. There are many potential crossovers that could lead to even more income.

If you have existing skills in the creative arts, business, retail or entrepreneurship these are absolutely transferable into digital passive income streams. So, it's time to start thinking about what products or services you could offer that will generate passive income online. There are many forms this can take which we will cover in-depth throughout the following section.

Remember that similar to the offline business world, not every idea you have necessarily have, has a pot of gold attached to the end of it. For the most part it's a learning curve as well as discovering new strategies, not to mention honing in on trends.

In many cases, it also takes careful thought and effort to get something truly up and running off the ground. Without further ado, let's take an in-depth look at some of the most popular sources of digital passive income.

YouTube

A video-sharing platform in the form of a website and app. Users can upload, comment, like and share videos, as well as embed videos on other websites.

You've probably heard of people making money off YouTube (https://creatoracademy.youtube.com/page/course/bootcamp-foundations) long before you bought this book. There are millions of people all across the world uploading video content to YouTube and making a profit off it.

When you upload videos onto YouTube, you have the option of monetizing your videos through Google Adsense. Every time someone views an advert that plays before or during your video you will earn a small percentage of that advertising revenue. You can also allow pop up adverts which will display in the bottom corner of your videos.

In order for your videos to become eligible to be monetized, there are some boxes that need to be ticked. You will first need to sign up for a Google Adsense account that is linked to your YouTube channel (https://www.youtube.com/watch?v=W4CjMJO_qcM). You will also need to have at least 1,000 subscribers and 4,000 hours of watch time before your videos are eligible for monetization.

Once you reach this point, your videos will need to comply with its advertising terms and conditions. If your videos are not deemed suitable (for example if they contain violence or profanity), then they could be demonetized.

If you are starting from scratch, getting 1,000 subscribers can seem like a tough gig. It goes without saying that YouTube is not the "get rich quick" scheme it appears to be. It does take regular uploads, great quality and a constant dedicated effort to start to see any real earnings. It is entirely possible if you're willing to put the work in.

YouTube is over a decade old and shows no sign of slowing down in the popularity stakes, despite fierce competition from other social media platforms.

The richest YouTubers according to moneyinc.com (https://moneyinc.com/richest-youtubers-in-2019) are as follows:

1. Jeffree Star - $75 Million
2. Daniel Middleton - $45 Million
3. Logan Paul - $40 Million
4. Markiplier - $24 Million
5. Ryan Toys Review - $22 Million
6. Jake Paul - $21.5 million
7. Dude Perfect - $20 Million
8. Pew Die Pie - $20 Million
9. John Green - $19 Million
10. Evan Fong - $17 Million
11. Lilly Singh - $16 Million
12. The German Garmendia - $13 Million
13. James Charles - $12 Million
14. Roman Atwood - $12 Million
15. Shane Dawson - $12 Million
16. Ninja - $10 Million
17. Ali A - $5 Million
18. Dolan Twins - $4 Million

19. Liza Koshy - $4 Million
20. Trisha Paytas - $4 Million

These people have made that amount of money for several reasons, mainly because they were smart about their strategy. Monetizing with ads at the start of the video and at several points throughout it. Selling merch, using affiliate links in the description and capitalizing on sponsorships and other opportunities that came their way.

There are many niches on YouTube that are pretty crowded (beauty and gaming for example). That's not to say you can't succeed in these categories, but it will take something very different for people to watch your content over beauty gurus with 10 million followers.

So what do you need to succeed on YouTube? It goes without saying that you need to have a good personality and be confident on camera. If you don't grab people's attention they quickly exit your video after just a few seconds, putting your efforts to waste. People will be unlikely to subscribe and that revenue won't roll in.

Don't be discouraged though, your skills can be developed even by rehearsing beforehand. Look at what the most popular YouTubers are doing and while it's not about straight-up copying anyone - it's worth understanding what makes a winning formula.

YouTube by its very nature is a visual platform. People want interesting content that grabs them. That includes a well-lit background, plenty of jump cuts and entertaining content.

If you are showing products, you should film close-ups from different angles. Make the experience as tangible as possible for your viewers. Remember there is a lot of competition out there, so give people excellently edited videos, clear sound and informative content.

Avoid long boring so-called "talking head" videos, which will leave people falling asleep, not subscribing. The frame should change to a different angle, close up or shoot every few frames to keep the viewers focused and interested in what you have to say.

Once you master these basics, you will start to build a community. The more people who subscribe to your content and ultimately view it, the more you will build a passive income. Those who have perfected this formula are the ones who have gone on to make YouTube their full-time careers.

You should always combine your videos with an excellent marketing strategy. This starts from having SEO in your titles, tags and subscriptions through to an active social media presence. Every time you post a video, it should go out on all social media channels. You can even use Hootsuite to repost links to your content every few hours, taking even less time and effort.

Another way you can earn money through YouTube is through affiliate links. These are specially created links that will earn you commission each time a sale is made. We will discuss affiliate links in greater detail throughout the next section.

Twitch

Did you know there is such a thing as being paid to sit at home and play games? You can do just that on a platform called Twitch.

You need just 50 followers to become a Twitch affiliate, meaning you can start to earn money just from playing games on the site (here's a guide to help you figuring out how https://www.tomsguide.com/us/twitch-streaming-guide,review-3009.html). It will give you a share of the pre-roll ads shown on your stream, similar to how YouTubers make money from ads that play alongside or before their videos.

One of the main ways to earn money through Twitch is by gaining subscriptions to your stream. Subscriptions cost between $4.99 and $24.99, and the streamer will get 50% of all money raised this way. If you built your stream up and got to 1,000 subscriptions, that would earn you between $29,940 and $149,940 a year depending on what level of subscription people took out.

In addition, views can also purchase 'bits', which are animated emojis that appear in the chat of your stream. Every time viewers purchase these bits, you'll receive a cut. Viewers can also donate money to you without subscribing, and this method gives you a 100% cut of the earnings.

Finally, you can also earn income on Twitch by using affiliates such as links or product placement. For example, you feature a specific keyboard or gaming chair on your channel for a fee. As your popularity grows, this method can become extremely lucrative.

There are people who have done very well out of streaming through Twitch. One such person is Ninja (https://www.twitch.tv/ninja), who earns $5,417,447 through all the different features including subscriptions and donations. So, if you have a knack for gaming or presenting then Twitch is definitely a passive income stream to consider.

5.1 Affiliate Marketing (Passive and Active)

Active Affiliate Definition: *Money given in return for links or advertising displayed on a website that generates a sale.*

Passive Affiliate Definition: *An online retailer pays commission to an external website for traffic or sales generated from its referral.*

Passive affiliate marketing is the process of earning a commission by promoting someone else's product or service. By promoting that service by what's known as an affiliate link, you will earn a commission every time that company makes a sale as a result. If you're new to passive affiliate marketing, click here to access a free guide (https://smartblogger.com/affiliate-marketing).

There are many different affiliate programs out there that will allow you to earn revenue. Most affiliate programs give people the ability to join for free, and promote their products to earn a commission. Or you can create your own Active Affiliate program, where people sell your products or services, and they earn from you a commission out of it. You can check out my affiliate program at my Shoes and Clothing online store dr3am1ng.com by clicking on "AFFILIATES" on the menu bar. See how easy it is to create?!

When you join a program (Passive Affiliate), you'll be given what's known as an affiliate link. This link will have a special format, and will allow the company to track how many sales you are making through it so you can earn your commission.

What makes passive affiliate marketing so great is that you don't have to create a product or service to earn revenue. Instead, your revenue is being earned by promoting other people's products and services. In fact, you don't even need to sell the product because once you've linked your friends, family, subscribers etc to the page, it is the page itself that will sell the product. You are simply endorsing the product through the link. No selling, postage, customer support, shipping or other hard work involved!

You're simply *sending* the traffic to the website where people can buy the product or service. All you need for that is the affiliate link, which you can either display under a video or on a social media post. Alternatively, you can create a backlink through your blog. For example, you are a beauty blogger who is promoting a Mac Cosmetics palette. Your readers can see you've inserted a link telling people where they can buy it. That link is affiliated, and when they go ahead and click on the link and also complete the purchase, you will be given a commission of that sale.

Affiliate marketing is always a win-win for everyone involved, both the active and passive investors. It's a win for the company, that will ultimately get more sales because you are sending traffic their way. This is a customer who probably wouldn't have made the sale without being directly linked through you. It's also a win for you because you will profit every single time someone buys the product through your link. Plus, it requires very little effort except signing up for the program and copying and pasting the link into your blog, video, website or social media posts.

You haven't had to invest capital, invent something or take a huge risk. You simply have copied and pasted a link and will benefit every time someone then goes onto make a purchase. Of course you will have to work on having a good audience, because the more people you have looking and clicking on that promo link, the more sales you will make, and the more revenue you will earn from the merchant.

Affiliate linking is indeed, closely related to the previous two categories: Blogging and YouTube. It does however require its own category to fully explain how it works. After all, there is potentially a lot of money to be made if you own a website, blog or YouTube channel. If you dream of cutting down the number of hours you work per work, then affiliate marketing could hold the key.

Examples of affiliate programs include Amazon, Awin, BlueHost, ClickBank, Commission Junkie, eBay Partners, FlexOffers, Max Bounty, Share A Sale, Shopify, Studio Press and many more. There are literally thousands and thousands! Try and sign up with as many as possible to increase your earning potential.

In essence, affiliate linking is where you link to another product or service through your content. This can take the form of a blog post or in your YouTube description box. If someone then makes a purchase of said product or service, then you will receive a commission from the company.

There are many different companies that offer affiliate linking, so it's worth shopping around to find the best commission rates. Stick to the merchants who are closely related to your topic area. The key is to create targeted posts that correspond with the rest of your website, as the more your viewers stay on your page and click the content, the more likely they are to make a purchase.

Similar to blogging and YouTube, affiliate linking also benefits from SEO content, and from social media marketing. After all, if people aren't landing on your content in the first place, you will not receive any click-through links to generate a sale.

Affiliate marketing is not just for bloggers either. Let's say you have a website that sells musical instruments, and you use affiliate links to paid courses that will teach people how to play the piano or guitar. Every time someone uses your link and then pays for that course, you will earn a commission.

It's a simple way that absolutely anyone can use to generate more income, without having to invest more capital in the business. It's also a win-win for you once again, because if people don't know how to play an instrument which is a barrier for them purchasing one from you, they are much more likely knowing they can access a course to learn how to.

Maybe you're into hair and beauty, but your site doesn't actually sell products it just gives advice. When you recommend people buy the Dyson Supersonic Hairdryer ($399) or the Jeffree Star Blood Sugar Palette ($96) through affiliate links, you're going to earn a commission every time you do. Even if the commission is just 10%, that's $39 and $9.60 a time respectively. Make just 1 affiliate sale per day and that would give you a total of $14,235 for the Dyson and $3,504 on these two items alone! Imagine if you put up 5+ similar blog posts a day, and sold more than 1 item a day? This is exactly how people are making such huge passive income from affiliate links alone.

Every affiliate will set their own rate, which tends to give more commission the more expensive the product or service is. For example, Trip Advisor will pay you 50% of their commission per confirmed booking through affiliate marketing. As Trip Advisor earns 10% of the total booking, this will give you 5% of the booking fee. For example, if a hotel stay is booked to the value of $1,000, Trip Advisor will get $100 of that money, which they will then split 50/50 with you, which is $50 each.

Say you have a fantastic review of a luxury hotel you stayed at, and the post got 10,000 views. Add $100 in targeted Facebook and Instagram ads and you will get 100,000 views. If only 1% of people go onto book, that's 1,000 lots of commission. If the average stay is $1,000 as it was in our above example, that would earn you $50,000 (the best scenario). Again divide it per 50% (a more conservative scenario) and it's $25,000. Plus, you can apply the same scheme for different hotels or even properties (Villas, Apartments etc.), with a view to increase exponentially that $25.000. Their program also offers banners and widgets to use on your site, meaning it really can become lucrative very quickly, if someone then goes onto book.

Don't get me wrong here. I know that nothing is that easy, but in reality it is all about knowledge and practice. If you keep on increasing your knowledge by becoming a perpetual learning machine, you are going to master SEO techniques, and the social media and content marketing strategies needed for targeted ads. The successful combination of these strategies can lead to incredible results.

Affiliate marketing is one of the few income streams that doesn't have any risk attached, which is one of the reasons it's so popular. Not only are there no start-up costs, but if it fails or takes a while for people to start using - it's not going to cost you money. It's also really easy to fix your strategy (SEO for one!) so that you are getting traffic to your website who will then go on to click the link.

If you use affiliate links it's always good to disclaim this somewhere within your website or description box. That way, you keep some transparency between your website and your readers.

◆ ◆ ◆

5.2 Pay Per Lead

A type of affiliate marketing program whereby financial compensation is offered in return for leads to that business .

Pay per lead (PPL) works on a similar premise to pay per click and affiliate marketing. As the name suggests, the company will pay you for leads for their business. Some either approach this by creating their own marketing agency, or by using existing PPL schemes.

Let's take Grammarly for example, who offer $25 for placing a banner on your website advertising their product. They will then give you 20 cents for every additional lead. If you run an educational website or even if you're in marketing, everyone could benefit from Grammarly as it's a super-easy way to spell check and improve documents. If your website gets 2,000 hits a day and 100 people sign up, that would earn you $20 a day, or $7,300 a year. There are also cash bonuses for the top affiliates.

Another great PPL scheme is Born To Sell, who are a software development firm that creates easy to use covered call investment tools. They offer $5 on all trials and $40 for each person who then goes on to buy the product. Their website states that 54% of all free trials go onto full subscriptions, earning an average of $26.50 per free sign up. In total, you could earn $45 per sign up. They allow PPL affiliate linking through social media, websites, blogs, social media pages and more. In addition, they supply you with 11 different assets to use on each of the different platforms. Click here to learn more and get started (https://www.borntosell.com/affiliates).

Going back to that $391 per stream a day needed to make $1,000,000 in 12 months, you'd need to get just over 8 successful leads per day from your website. Again it's not easy, but it's absolutely possible! Remember that PPL is just one form of passive income within one revenue stream. It definitely shows the potential though, especially when you have to do absolutely nothing other than display a banner on your website.

Some set up their own PPL agency, charging $35 per lead aiming to deliver 100 leads per company per day. That would generate $3,500 per day, or $1,277,500 per year. If the leads were coming from ads, banners and links in evergreen content that's entirely plausible. Remember, PPL is not the same as cold calling! It can come from static digital content and is generating millions of leads for businesses every single day. The more leads generated = the more commission you make.

5.3 Sell Digital Assets

Definition: *Digital media such as photography, video, music or art, that can be sold for profit.*

If you're a creative individual you might already have thousands of potential assets you could sell online to create a digital passive income. If you're not creative, why not use a freelancing platform and get someone else to create assets for you?

A very popular choice is t-shirt designs which can be turned around quickly by a designer, and uploaded onto many of the online print stores such as Teespring or Redbubble. This is known as print on demand (or POD). There is always going to be a demand for clothing and if your t-shirts offer creativity or humor, or just all-round quality then they are likely to get snapped up. Plus, with this method there is no investment, other than the designs as the products are printed on demand by an external company.

Stock websites exist because people sell their photography and video content to them. Although the return isn't huge for photography, it's a return none the less. If you are a skilled video editor and you're able to make intros or transitions that other creators can use, you may find you're able to earn much more.

Even if you're just an amateur, if you have pictures or video you can sell to stock websites, it's going to be worth your time. Shutterstock pays between 25-38 cents per download. If you really get yourself established as a contributor, you'll start to command the higher threshold of 38 cents per download.

Let's crunch some numbers here. Say you upload 100 images onto Shutterstock over the space of a year. If each image is downloaded 1,000 times (it's a stock website with 1.4 million users, it's entirely plausible!) - that would earn you $38,000 a year.

But it's not just going to reach a cut-off point at the end of the year. If these images continue to be popular as they already have been, this income will continue to increase. Say things dip a little, look at what is trending and take some more photos.

Before you submit content, take a look at what is popular versus what there is a demand for but there is little supply of here in Shutterstock.com (https://www.shutterstock.com/explore/contributor-success-guide-core). The last thing you want to do is upload generic content that gets looked over or even rejected. Always submit high-resolution images and if applicable, upload your content in different resolutions and file formats. The more people who can access your content, the more likely it is to be downloaded earning you a profit each time.

Remember that stock websites are not just about finding people wearing suits shaking hands. Think about how the world of work is changing. We're *all* trying to ditch the office somehow, hence why you're even reading this book in the first place! So, what does that mean in terms of the images you need to take to earn a decent amount of passive income from the royalties?

Think about cool people. The offices with biophilia (plants!). Managers who wear jeans and a t-shirt. Find what the modern office really looks like, how people are earning their money these days. It's not just sitting behind a computer in a stale office block with magnolia walls. People want tangible, relatable images they can use for their marketing and social media campaigns.

There is also a huge demand nowadays for photos to use on social media pages. There's a lot of amateur photos rather than highly professional ones. So there is space for everything. Once again make your own content and check what are the most searched subjects (keywords) on stock websites.

For example, check here what are the most downloaded stock images of the year (https://www.stockphoto-secrets.com/stock-agency-insights/most-downloaded-images--2018.html). For the most part, you'll notice it's images which can be used for a variety of industries. Anything too niche is unlikely to be used, so stick with popular trends.

If you have some little capital to invest, you could even hire such a space as well as models (who will need to sign a model release form for stock website use). Say the shoot costs $1,000-$2,000 tops to create your 100 images. If it's earning you a potential of $38,000 a year it's easy money. Apply the same formula for lots of different scenarios depending on what stock websites are in short supply of (do your research). Do the work once and keep making money from that single one-time effort.

You can also sell fonts and creative templates. There are lots of websites that facilitate this including portfolio websites. Click here for an excellent article by Creative Bloq (https://www.creativebloq.com/typography/how-sell-your-type-faces-61620752) to point you in the right direction. If you're a designer or typographer with a high profile view count, use this to your advantage and sell some assets. You can also create tutorials on creative techniques or how to guides.

People are always going to need fonts, illustrations and even customizable downloads. Think about all the marketing agencies that suddenly need an infographic but don't have the time or the talent to design one. Could you make one on your website that can be easily customized?

If you were to make a custom font for a client, you could in effect charge thousands of dollars. But, this would take a lot of time and would be classed as active income rather than passive. If you're a struggling illustrator trying to get away from demanding clients, this is not the avenue to take.

The passive alternative is to create a series of downloadable fonts. You can either create your own website for this which will take time to market, but you'll keep all the royalties, or use one of a number of font selling websites. Examples include Hype For Type, My Fonts or You Work For Them.

Selling your own font via these websites can earn you between $20-$180 per download. So, just by selling 10 fonts at somewhere in the middle, say $100, that would earn you $1,000, or $12,000 worth of passive income every year. That's just from one font! If you could make 5 equally successful fonts, that would be $60,000 of passive income a year. You can have more designers to work on it, hired on Upwork and Fiverr. Again, look to scale the business and increase the profit by 3 or 4 times.

If you really want to hit the jackpot, you can't just rush in with a terrible product. Anyone who has studied graphic design or typography will tell you that creating a font is a real art form. People are passionate about their lettering which is why they pay top dollar for it. If the words "kerning" and "tracking" are alien to you, then you've got a lot to learn.

If you're an entrepreneur with no creative ability at all, reach out to a designer on Upwork and make it happen. Ad agencies around the world will snap up your product if it really is good enough. Look at what typographic styles are in demand and just go for it.

Onto something a little more melodic, and you don't need a record deal anymore to make and release your own music. There are countless streaming services or stock music websites you can upload your tunes onto for a fee. If you already have a following on social media it's worth uploading your music for paid download. However, you may find more commercial success with stock music as millions of people require music for their videos, presentations, advertisements and more.

Some of the best-known stock music websites include Audio Network, The Music Case, Pond5 and Tune Core. Another is Audio Jungle, who sell music and sound clips for an average of $1-$30. Say you start off with a low price of $5 for a piece of upbeat corporate music. Sell that piece of music 100 times and that's $500 of passive income. Sell a bundle including different track lengths or variations for $30. Make 100 sales and you'll have earned $3,000.

The great thing about these audio websites is you can literally sell anything that is a sound. Dogs barking, leaves rustling and even applause are all sounds. Think of someone editing a movie that needs a door creaking open. Do you have a microphone and a creaky door? Go make some money off it. Even if it's just $1 a download, that's still more that you had before. If it's a really great sound or piece of music, it's going to attract a lot of downloads.

Click here for a free guide (https://badgrammrbaz.com/sell-your-music-online) about how to start selling your music online.

❖ ❖ ❖

5.4 Sell Physical Products

If you're serious about passive income, then it's time to claim your slice of the online retail pie. If you have previous experience running or store or none at all - now's the time to hone your skills and create an online store. Even if you've never sold a thing in your life... you can still do it!

You need to decide on a niche. What products are you going to sell, and who is your target demographic? For example, you sell toys and your products are aimed at children aged 5-12. Once you have this groundwork in place, you'll then need to develop a marketing strategy. The more people who know about your website, the more likely it is you will make sales.

Just like a regular retail store, you're going to need to buy stock. This can be a huge upfront cost, so you might want to start small with just a few products to begin with. Depending on what you're selling, you'll also need a space to store your items in. You'll also need to work out postage and shipping, as well as your returns policy.

Amazon FBA (fulfillment by Amazon) is by far the best way of selling products, especially if you are a newly established (or almost) brand. The benefit of selling through Amazon is that it's one of the most popular websites in the world, therefore has an extremely large audience. Quite simply, Amazon FBA takes your existing business model but makes it more visible to more customers.

You'll need to send your inventory to selected Amazon stores around the world (or only in the US if you prefer), where it will be stored securely by Amazon (you can send as little or as much stock as you want). When customers then go to buy your products, Amazon will take care of all the handling and shipping, as well as customer service and returns. In essence, it's a way of supersizing your brand by selling your products through Amazon, without the hassle of individually processing each order yourself. Kick start here your Amazon selling through Jungle Scout guide on "how to" and their tools. (https://www.junglescout.com)

Fees cost between $1 per item or $39 a month for a professional subscription to Amazon FBA. While $468 a year might sound like a lot, for the sheer amount of customers you can reach through Amazon (estimated at over 300 million customers worldwide, of which 100 million are Prime customers) it's definitely worth it. That being said, you need to have a profitable business model before you start, as anyway the competition is very fierce.

Manny Coates is just one extremely successful case study. Check it out here (https://www.ampmpodcast.com/about-manny-coats). He made $1,000,000 through Amazon FBA in just 9 months! I highly suggest checking his story out to study his technique.

If you're not planning on selling through Amazon, you will need to purchase a website and a domain. Obviously you can have both, as it's always better to diversify the sales channels. You can either build this yourself or use a platform such as Shopify. There's no right or wrong here, but beware that many online retail platforms will charge a commission on each sale, or at least a monthly fee. Shopify for example charges $29 a month. Make sure you've researched the costings before you sign up, so you can really get your business off the ground.

Visually your store needs to be easy to navigate, and your products should have a logical order. People like to see clear images of products taken from different angles. For example, if you're selling clothing, make sure you photograph each item on a model or mannequin as well as on its own. Or, for a beauty store be sure to swatch products clearly so people understand what they are buying and whether it would be suitable for them.

Always write detailed descriptions about your products, including details about the materials and sizes. The better the customer experience you provide, the more likely you are to secure repeat business. Combining your online store with visible links to social media will help grow your business even more. More customers = more sales. You know what that means right? More income.

While there is undoubtedly a lot of work that goes into an online store (although not with Shopify or Amazon), it's a great way to create a brand. For the most part, the beginning stages of creating your store will fall into the 'active income' side of things. But as time progresses you will be able to maintain your store with ease. You can even outsource freelancers to run your store and take care of your customer service. This will definitely shift things back into the passive income stakes.

5.5 Drop Shipping

Definition: *A method of selling online whereby the store doesn't keep the products it sells in stock. Instead, when a customer orders a product it is actually handled from a 3rd party. As a result, the original seller never sees or handles the product.*

Starting an online business isn't always practical. You need a great idea, stock not to mention a place to store said stock. It can make creating your online store really difficult, not least because it requires a mostly active approach, rather than passive.

This is where Drop shipping comes in. Drop shipping allows you to sell products without ever having to physically handle them yourself. So, no buying stock or needing warehouse space. All you need is your computer, a website and a basic understanding of how to market a business.

First, identify what niche you want to go into. What exactly is it you want to sell? Find this, and then get yourself one or more suppliers who can provide the goods. You'll then list the products on your website, at a cost that you decide. When a customer orders, they will pay the price you set and you'll make a profit. You'll then place the order with your supplier at wholesale price, who will then ship the product directly to your customer.

So, let's say you found an essential oil set on your supplier's website for $30, and you list it on your website for $50. When the order comes through, you'd then place that order on your supplier's website using your customer's information, and you'd keep that $20 profit.

Naturally, you might think: "Why wouldn't the customer just order it from the original website?" Well, given there are over 1.5 billion websites that currently exist, it's a very big internet! Your customer isn't always going to be able to find your supplier's website, especially if the website isn't well known and their SEO isn't up to scratch. Plus, most of the time the manufacturer is only OEM, and so does not sell directly to end user like you do.

Another reason is that the product is a big part of the sales experience, but it isn't everything. Think about if you were to buy a designer pair of shoes. You're not just buying the shoes for the sake of it. You're buying into the marketing, the idea, the communication and what it represents etc. If your supplier isn't generally the same kind of excitement and ideal through their website, they aren't going to make the same level of sales.

With drop shipping, you can create a marketing strategy that works better than the original seller. This is because you will focus only on that specific aspect, without thinking about the manufacturing side. You can create that lifestyle and aesthetic that's missing and claim the profit along the way. After all, if you're not a big design house or a large fashion company - you're not dealing with day to day challenges most businesses have. That way, you don't have to worry about dropping the ball like they clearly have done. Essentially, you can sell their items even better than they do, with none of the cost or responsibility.

Even better, you can (I would say you MUST..) also create your own products, aka print on demand (POD products). This is a system that allows merchants to personalize products, drastically reducing competition. For example, you upload a t-shirt design to Redbubble who then takes care of all the customer service, ordering, manufacturing, printing, shipping and delivery for you. Compared to taking all of that on yourself as a budding designer, there are a lot less risks, not to mention costs.

Like all income streams, there are some challenges you're going to need to factor in before you start. Firstly, when you're drop shipping on your own you can spend a lot of time researching suppliers. So, if you're completely new to drop shipping you might want to check out an agency that will give you direct access to millions of products to sell, such as Wiio (https://www.wiio.io), who deal specifically with Chinese suppliers where most of the world's products are made.

Drop shipping is a popular passive income method, because it's really easy to get started. You can find out everything you need to know about getting started through this free guide here (https://www.shopify.com/guides/dropshipping). Drop shipping has incredibly low investment costs. You don't have to worry about managing inventory, which can be one of the biggest stresses of any online or physical retail store. Packing and tracking are also taken care of for you, meaning even less stress. Again with Shopify here, as it's a one-stop solution for your drop shipping business.

The biggest advantage is setting your own retail price. Going back to my essential oil example, and if you sold 1,000 units, that would give you $20,000 of pure profit. Remember, not only do you set the prices but you also set the niche too. You can pick exactly what's trending and what people want. You also don't have to deal with any of the frustrating, time-consuming actions in between. The money is also given to you before passing it onto your suppliers, meaning no buying stock without being directly paid for it first (earning a profit every time you do so!)

To make your drop shipping even more passive, you can hire virtual assistants to take care of the marketing and ordering for you. If you start to scale your business, this really makes sense. Plus, you can easily hire assistants on Upwork.com or on Fiverr.com in all corners of the globe, making your drop shipping business truly international. Although the amount of effort needed to run this business successfully is really small, I would still recommend doing everything on your own.

Some hurdles to overcome include if the supplier ships the wrong product to your customer. This scenario is highly rare, but it doesn't help to be prepared for the few times it might happen to you. If your customer receives the wrong item, it's important to stay calm and provide great customer service.

Only choose suppliers who offer refunds, which you can receive by providing photos of the wrong product, without the need for a return. You then simply need to order a new product with your supplier using their customer care service, by providing the pictures. Organize a new shipment to your customer or provide them with a refund (according to client choice) after the supplier has refunded you. There is usually a rating system for every supplier, which is very reliable if you use Shopify.

Since many suppliers are based in China, you're going to need to factor in shipping times for when people are placing orders with you. To avoid frustrating customers or losing sales, always clarify the shipping times clearly in your product descriptions before they buy and provide different types of shipments. Slow (better because it's free of charge) or fast with an extra charge.

Getting started is really simple. You can get a free 14 day trial on Shopify, which is the leading website for creating your own online store. Use an app such as Oberlo (https://www.oberlo.com) which will give you drop shipping products to import into your store. You'll then need to enable payment methods on your store, so that you can start accepting money and processing orders.

Next comes your marketing strategy. After all, no matter how good your store is, if nobody can find it then you won't make any sales. Your store needs to have a logical order, great product photography as well as SEO-rich descriptions. You need to then promote your store through as many mediums as possible. For example, have a blog on your website and link it to your store. Set up social media accounts linking to your store, as well as creating Google Ads. The more traffic you can generate, the more sales you will get too.

According to Niche Pursuits (https://www.nichepursuits.com/money-make-dropshipping), those who focus on high ticketed drop shipping will earn between $300 and $5,000 per day. Cutting that somewhere in the middle at $2,500 a day, that would earn you an average of $912,500 a year! Once again we have several examples of people who actually reached those goals, showing how it really is possible.

Niche Pursuits raise a good issue however, and that is your total income depends on not only how good your store concept, layout and marketing is, but also the relationship you build with your suppliers. That's why before jumping into drop shipping, it's worth doing your research or taking a free course to learn the ins and outs of how the industry works.

All the same, drop shipping remains one of the best sources of passive income. If you are really looking to scale your wealth, it should be one of your top considerations for your next revenue streams. As far as passive income goes, it's one of the easiest ways to get your $391 a day, as part of your 7 overall income streams to earn you $1,000,000 a year.

For an excellent case study example, check out here Andreas Koenig and Alexander Pecka who have succeeded in the pet niche through Oberlo (https://www.oberlo.com/blog/successful-pet-business). The more you can learn from those who have made drop shipping work, the more successful you will be.

5.6 Blogging

Definition: *A website that acts as an online journal. A blog can cover a variety of topics and is often interlaced with visual content and links to other websites.*

When anyone mentions the term digital passive income, one of the top strategies that spring to mind is blogging, and for good reason.

Blogging has been popular for quite some time now and has literally turned into full time careers for millions around the world. Similarly to YouTube earning model, blogging generates income through a combination of advertising, affiliate linking and sponsorship deals. Many bloggers have even become celebrities releasing books and other merchandise.

Blogging is a crowded market so it goes without saying that you'll need to bring something different to the table, especially if you are looking to blog about beauty or lifestyle. Click here some excellent free advice from Smart Blogger to point you in the right direction (https://smartblogger.com/how-to-write-a-blog-post). In addition, you'll need an active presence on social media, as well as a great looking website.

The key is to have as many people land on your content as possible. Fundamentally this comes from having a great writing style that is SEO heavy. If you're starting from scratch with no initial audience, getting to grips with SEO couldn't be more important. Don't forget social media and content marketing too!

If you own your own business, blogging can even help with your active income too. SEO rich content such as blogs are incredibly effective at bringing in traffic from search engines directly onto your website. Posting regular blogs helps drive your rankings up even further, because search engines do not like linking to stale websites with old content. So, not only can you earn money from advertising on your blog, you can also use it as an effective marketing strategy. If you're not a skilled wordsmith or don't have time to write your blogs, you can even hire a freelancer to do it for you.

The key to making money with blogging is delivering quality content in terms of both text and image quality. You need to tap into exactly what people are typing in the search bar so that they land on your content. Once they are there, you need to make them stay.

So, let's take a look at the most successful blogs (https://www.forbes.com/sites/robertadams/2017/03/02/top-income-earning-blogs/#2304b5672377) as reported by Forbes, along with how much they make per MONTH:

1. Huffington Post - $14,000,000
2. Engadget - $5,550,000
3. Moz - $4,250,000
4. Mashable - $2,000,000
5. TechCrunch - $2,500,000
6. CopyBlogger - $1,000,000
7. Perez Hilton - $575,000
8. Gizmodo - $325,000
9. Smashing Magazine - $215,000
10. Tuts+ - $175,000

Cast your eye down the list and you'll notice a bit of a repeating pattern here - news websites. While news is not the only profitable topic to blog about, it does represent a change in culture that also ties in with our previous discussion about procrastination.

In the old days we'd read about local and world events through a newspaper, right? Over the last couple of decades (since the internet really took off), the way we are consuming information is changing, and that couldn't be more true for news.

We all want to know what's happening in the world. Whether it's breaking news or celebrity gossip - there is a huge consumption for it that is growing at a rapid pace. Tie in the fact we use social media to share news stories, and the popularity of a single news story can go global in seconds.

News sites are big business, and so is the advertising revenue and affiliate linking that can be made from the profits. Every single click on your website can be translated into income, and the world can't get enough of it.

The Huffington Post is generating $168,000,000 a year. Visiting it to see what they are doing right would be an excellent place to start if you are thinking of following in their footsteps.

It goes without saying that with that kind of revenue they have access to the best journalists not to mention technology to give their users instant content. They even customize the website depending on your location, giving it a global feel.

Here are some takeaways to use in your blog, whether you have the budget of The Huffington Post, or if you are starting from absolute scratch:

Clean Graphics: It's not 1999 anymore, so stop it with the black background against red comic sans text. If you are serious about blogging, the visuals need to be clean and slick. Notice how THP uses razor-sharp photography in an easy to follow layout. Every part of their website is straightforward to navigate.

Regularly Updated: Google hates recommending content that's stale. News websites have an upper advantage here because someone is behind the scenes adding new content every second. Even if your blog isn't news-related, don't let content dry up. Schedule posts in advance so that fresh content is going up weekly, if not daily.

SEO: Search engine optimization is what links people searching on Google with your content. News websites use SEO in every single aspect of their content, from the headline to the picture captions, and of course several times throughout the text. If you've never heard of SEO before, take a free course on YouTube, or buy books about it. Like most of today's online technologies, it is something that everyone can learn pretty easily.

Easy social sharing: It needs to be made as easy as possible for people to share your content on social media. The more shares it receives, the more reads and the more revenue generated. If social media channels are nowhere to be seen under the article to directly share it, forget about ever having a chance to compete with the big boys in the list above.

Video content: You can earn way more advertising revenue if you have videos to accompany your articles. You can either run ads before and after the video, or use pop-up video advertising. Be aware that the latter isn't as successful these days due to people installing pop-up blockers.

Now we've covered the top blogging sites of all time according to revenue, how about the individual bloggers who've made it to the big time from these websites?

This is who they are and how much they earn per MONTH:

1. Arriana Huffington - Huffington Post: $41,000,000
2. Peter Rojas - Engadget: $3,950,000
3. Rand Fishkin - Moz: $3,740,000
4. Peter Cashmore - Mashable: $3,330,000
6. Brian Clark - CopyBlogger: $2,750,000
6. Michael Arrington - TechCrunch: $1,870,000
7. Perez Hilton - Perez Hilton: $575,000
8. Peter Rojas - Gizmodo: $541,000
9. Vitaly Friedman - Smashing Magazine: $430,000
10. Cyan Claire - Tuts+: $175,000

Next time someone rolls their eyes at you for starting a blog because there is "no money in it," be sure to show them this list!

For the most part, this group of people seized an opportunity. None of them started earning millions of dollars a year on their blog. They grew it through hard work and strategy, and that is the core of any financial venture you plan on making a success.

To get started you're going to need a catchy name that has a corresponding free domain (always check this before you go ahead). You can use GoDaddy's domain checker for free (www.godaddy.com/domains/domain-name-search) to make sure your dream name isn't already taken.

The topic you choose can literally be anything, but avoid topics that are too niche or where there is quite a bit of investment involved to start. For example, beauty blogs are popular but it requires buying all of the products to photograph and review. Only a small percentage make it to the point where they are sent free samples, so otherwise they have to absorb the cost themselves. This can end up costing you way more money than you'd ever make from your blog, so pick your theme wisely.

There are loads of websites where you can start your blog. Wordpress has some of the best themes, but beware that the original www.wordpress.com which is totally free, has quite a few limitations and drawbacks. For example, you will not be able to use premium domain names. It's also worth mentioning that Automatic (WordPress.com owner) will display their own ads on your website. The more advanced solutions require a premium subscription that's $300+ a year. If you have no idea what you're doing and have to pay a developer, it could work out to be even more expensive.

That's not to exclude Wordpress altogether as it remains one of the most popular blogging platforms. It's more to make sure you don't throw a tonne of money at a website with no concrete plan to generate revenue. It's really worth checking out alternatives such as wordpress.org, Spotify, Blogger, Tumblr, Medium, and Squarespace.

In fact, Squarespace and Shopify are around $29 a month, plus they are both user-friendly. Find the features and the plan that's right for you, and don't get sucked in for paying for premium features you'll never use.

Once you are set up with your platform and your domain,

you're going to need content. You can either hire someone on Upwork or Fiverr to write this for you, or do it yourself depending on how much time you have, and if you have the budget for outside help.

Start by writing at least 8 blogs in advance, so that you can schedule a minimum of 2 to go out per week. If you have more time, you can create more content than this. If you're setting up a news style website, you're going to need at least 5-10 stories a day as news gets stale very quickly.

Try and write posts that are around 500-1000 words. If the content is below 150 words, this is bad for SEO. Another factor that's going to help with SEO is spacing your content out neatly with video or images. You can use Pexels or Unsplash for images that are free to use commercially.

Ultimately, running a successful and profitable blog comes down to knowing your audience. Almost every blog platform will come with free analytical tools. It will tell you not just how many visitors are on your site, but also what they are searching for to reach you. This is a great indicator as to what is working (and what you should do more of) versus what's not working (what you should stop).

5.7 Write One Or More Ebooks (Self Publish)

Gone are the days where you need to submit writing examples to publishers in the faint hope of securing a book deal. These days you can become your very own publishing house. One of the easiest ways to do this is by writing an ebook.

Due to the popularity of both nonfiction and fiction ebooks, it can become a great source of passive income. Amazon currently offers 70% royalties on all ebooks sold, and given there are well over 300 million users on the site, that's a lot of potential readers. Other notable ebook sites include Weebly, Nook Press and Smashwords.

Before you type a single word, you need to put in some research. Take a look at Amazon Kindlestore and similar ebook sites. It's important to look at topics and authors who are doing well alongside those who aren't. You need to understand what will really make people want to buy your book before you put the effort into writing it.

Firstly decide on a topic (don't worry if you don't have the title just yet). You need to understand exactly what the book is going to be about from the offset. Who is your target audience, and what message do you want to get across? There is little point in writing a book if this is not clear, as if it doesn't even make sense to you, it's doubtful it will to your audience either.

A good place to start is the Amazon book chart (https://www.amazon.com/Best-Sellers-Books/zgbs/books). You'll notice a variety of niches from celebrity life stories to cookery books and even kid's books. There is no set theory on what works best, but it goes without saying that you're going to need to put some thought and research into your finished product before you get started.

Then you will need to plan the structure using a combination of chapters and headings. You may wish to make notes under each heading so when you get to that section, you at least have an idea where to start. Like any good story there should be a clear beginning, middle and end.

Whilst there will be some formatting to contend with, you can write your ebook on virtually any software. Google Docs is an excellent free resource, and it's also great to oversee your ghostwriter or editor. You can add comments to sections that need changes and see realtime progress. It also automatically saves so no corrupt files or broken hard drive horrors to deal with!

Onto the visuals and as the saying goes "Don't just a book by its cover" - in reality a poorly designed ebook cover could mean people overlook it in favor of another author. If you're not a graphic designer don't worry! You can outsource this to a local agency or a freelancing website. The cover is very important. So outsourcing the design of it is a must. Make it beautiful and clear, and always keep in mind that Amazon has a white background, so do not make a white cover, but one which colors stand out.

It's helpful to provide the designer with a brief overview of the synopsis, as well as an idea of what you want it to look like. Be sure to allow them some creative freedom as graphic designers are incredibly experienced visual artists. Great communication is key, as your ebook cover has an awful lot of competition.

When it comes to pricing your ebook, you might be surprised to hear it can actually pay off if the price is quite low. If you're an unheard of author and you don't have a solid marketing strategy, it's unlikely anyone is going to jump in and paid $19.99 a time for your ebook. Pricing it at $2.99 might seem unreasonable, but it's a great way to attract sales. Once you've built a loyal audience, you can then look to increase this figure.

Like all forms of passive income, ebooks are a learning curve. It's all about pitching the right idea, offering the audience a great story or inspirational journey they will want to stick with the whole way through. Whether you are writing a short story (under 10,000 words) or even a series of novels, publishing an ebook is a great source of passive income that virtually anyone can do.

Follow the above advice and aim to make $20,000 a month by writing a series of ebooks. Research and write great content, create and implement a marketing strategy. Once again do not forget that searches on Amazon work per keywords, so it is essential to make a search on the most researched keywords and use those for your topics, your title and your description. Again SEO makes the difference.

Once you've achieved that, you will be earning $240,000 a year on ebook sales alone. This is almost a quarter of the way to reaching 7 figures without taking into account your other income streams.

Amazon Kindle has now also an integrated service which allows you to print on demand and ship directly from Amazon itself your ebook. So you can have your paperback version of it printed and shipped directly by Amazon.

5.8 Books Self-Publishing

Book publishing can be both digital (see the section on e-books), however, traditional book publishing is still a viable way of earning passive income.

If you've always had a great story just waiting to be told, then becoming a novelist can really pay off. If you are knowledgeable in a subject such as medicine, science, politics, language, fitness etc - you could also put pen to paper and release your own book related to your specialism. Check out this free simple guide to publish your book in 7 easy steps (https://blog.reedsy.com/how-to-self-publish-a-book).

You could choose to self publish or go through a publishing house. It can be difficult to score a book deal and so most choose to self publish. Both have pros and cons when it comes to marketing and royalties.

You're going to need to establish the cost of writing, printing and distributing your book. You'll also need someone to design the cover, as well as develop a marketing strategy. If you go with a publisher they will take care of this for you, but this means they will take a cut from your royalties, plus they will own the copyright.

According to Wealthy Gorilla (https://wealthygorilla.com/richest-authors-world), these are the richest authors of all time:

1. Elisabeth Badinter - $1.3 billion
2. J.K Rowling - $1 billion

3. James Patterson - $560 million
4. Stephen King - $400 million
5. Nora Roberts - $390 million
6. Danielle Steele - $310 million
7. Barbara Taylor Bradford - $300 million
8. Nigel Blackwell - $292.5 million
9. John Grisham - $220 million
10. Jeffrey Archer - $195 million

There is money to be made in books because there is always room for new stories, just like there is for music, tv shows and movies. Whether you are a fiction or non-fiction writer, if you have a story in you there is little point keeping it in your head if you want to make money from it!

Take J.K Rowling who is second on the list as an example. She was a struggling author who was broke, trying to support her kid when she got the idea for Harry Potter. J.K even escaped domestic violence at the time, and in a documentary about her life it showed a scene where she chose between a typewriter to create her first draft and food.

While that's an extreme example, it shows that even if you are facing hardship you can still go onto make it. Because J.K was determined to write her story and get it published (she faced endless rejection, FYI!) she's now a billionaire.

It all comes back to that mindset of being determined to succeed and working hard until you do. Book publishing is no different, where you are going to self publish or try and get a book deal - write your best work, and don't give up until you make it.

◆ ◆ ◆

5.9 Create An Audiobook

Together with writing an ebook, keep always in mind to add the audible version of it. There is a lot less competition on audiobooks, and sometimes audiobooks can make you earn even more than the classic ebooks.

For those who don't have time to read a whole ebook, audiobooks are a great alternative. The beauty of audiobooks is you can listen to them in the car on the way to work, while you're working out in the gym or even before you go to bed at night. In this modern age people are busy and so multitasking is a must, which is what makes audiobooks so great. Audiobooks are also an excellent resource for the visually impaired.

You can also sell your audiobook through Amazon's "books on CD" (https://www.amazon.com/Best-Sellers-Books-CD/zgbs/books/69724/ref=zg_bs_nav_b_1_b) section. At the time of writing the best selling audiobooks are selling through this platform for between $7 and $51. There is of course the better known Audible (https://www.audible.com/ep/memberbenefits), which offers 40% royalties for all retail sales through Audible, Amazon, and iTunes.

Say you sold your audiobook at $19.99, that would make you $7.99 per sale. Say you combined that with Amazon's suggested marketing strategy (https://www.acx.com/help/

promote-yourself/200485310), and your audiobook really took off, selling 500 copies a month. That would earn you $3,999 a month or $47,988 a year.

Plus, Amazon will also give you $75 for every new listener you bring to Audible (https://www.acx.com/help/bounty-referral-program/UEF9JUCH9AZEKA4). Say you bring 100 new listeners through your book, blog or vlog. That will earn you an additional $7,500 in a space of a year. Your total earnings for your audiobook would then be $55,488. Write and record one book every 3 months and following the exact same aggressive marketing strategy to give you the same results. That would earn you $221,952 a year.

So, what makes a great audiobook? (https://self-publishingschool.com/creating-audiobook-every-author-know) Well, take a look at the current Audiobook charts (https://www.amazon.com/Best-Sellers-Books-Audible-Audiobooks/zgbs/books/2402172011) and familiarise yourself with the best sellers. What do they have that you can replicate in your own way? It's not about copying (that could land you in hot water anyway). It's about finding what makes a successful story when recorded.

Speaking of recording, you'll also need to find a great narrator unless you are able to do this yourself. This will incur an upfront fee, as will designing a great cover for your audiobook to display on Amazon or similar websites. But, without these elements being delivered to the right standard you won't make any sales so don't go too cheap on this.

5.10 Build An Online Course

Definition: *A way of learning a new skill or talent through digital means.*

We briefly mentioned this under sell digital assets, and this is one passive income stream that can really earn big bucks. If you have a talent or skill, why don't you share it with the world?

Designing, musical instruments, illustration, coding, entrepreneurship, language lessons, survival skills, home improvements, cooking - the list is literally endless. Plus, the exact same subjects can go into your blog generating even more income.

There are a lot of skill-sharing websites where you can develop your own course. Another idea would be to build your own (check here how https://www.learnworlds.com/how-to-create-an-online-course), therefore retaining more of the profit. Granted, this would have required an initial fee to pay each of the guests not to mention put together a slick production. But, it's a formula that clearly works as a brilliant source of passive income for the CEO.

If you don't have the budget, why not sell your own story? If you've got an inspiring story or have built up a business from scratch people will want to know about it. You could even connect with other business leaders or people from your professional and create your very own series. It's about being inventive while inspiring people to learn new skills or strategies.

Building an online course may take time, but the process is straightforward. Say you want to teach people how to use SEO to market their business. This might be a competitive market, but there is definitely a demand for it. After all, not all business owners have the resources to hire someone to do their marketing for them, given the average marketing manager salary in the US is $145,620. There is no way a start-up can afford that! So, entrepreneurs and business owners look for a course they can take instead.

Say you create a 6 part course that people can buy as individual episodes for $50 or as a bundle for $250. You entice them with great taglines to make them want to part with their cash, and have a great marketing strategy including the odd bit of clickbait. If you can sell your course to just 2 people a day, that would earn you $500, which is well over the $391 a day target for your individual income stream to make $2,740 a day, in order to make $1,000,000 a year.

Remember, your course is completely passive other than reviewing the marketing strategy and giving some customer support (you can always outsource these tasks too). If you can sell your marketing course to 2 people a day, that would give you $182,500 a year... and that's just 2 sales of one course! Say you expanded it to include other forms of marketing or business management and created 10 courses at the same pricing of $50 per lesson or $250 per bundle.

If you only sold 1 course a day from each category, that would earn you $2,500 a day, which is almost your entire $2,740 a day target to reach $1,000,000 a year. Over the space of a year, that $2,500 would equate to $912,500... almost your $1,000,000 right there! Impossible? No. Tough? Yes.. But it just takes a lot of knowledge and smart work!!

According to Forbes, Coursera's revenue (https://www.class-central.com/report/coursera-2018-revenue-140-million) for 2018 was $140 Million, up from $100 Million in 2017. Udacity's revenue (https://www.classcentral.com/report/udacity-2018-review) grew by 25% to $90 million, and edX (https://www.insidehighered.com/digital-learning/article/2018/12/18/quest-long-term-sustainability-edx-tries-monetize-moocs) was at around $60 million. In terms of users, Coursera leads with 37 million, followed by edX ($18 million), XuetangX ($14 million), Udacity ($10 million) and FutureLearn ($8.7 million).

With an aggressive marketing strategy, the right presentation, excellent reviews, word of mouth, social media marketing etc - there is absolutely no reason why you can't hit that target, especially if you know what you are talking about. If it's something people desperately need to learn to keep their business afloat, or even if it's just a hobby like teaching someone to play a musical instrument - so long as there is a demand, you can be the supplier.

A good place to start is to look at the best selling courses on Udemy (https://www.udemy.com). As per the latest figures, these are the best-rated courses for 2019:

1. The Web Developer Bootcamp
Cost: $261
Students enrolled: 493,535
Total: $128,812,635

2. Complete Python Bootcamp
Cost: $255
Students enrolled: 766,050

Total: $195,342,750

3. Entire MBA in 1
Cost: $261
Students enrolled: 277,064
Total: $72,313,704

4. Digital Marketing: 12 Courses in 1
Cost: $261
Students enrolled: 321,105
Total: $83,808,405

5. Excel for Beginners to Advanced
Cost: $196
Students enrolled: 283,065
Total: $46,660,740

6. Hands-On Artificial Neural Networks
Cost: $261
Students enrolled: 192,539
Total: $50,252,679

7. Financial Analyst 2018
Cost: $255
Students enrolled: 152,775
Total: $38,957,625

8. Free courses provided by Udemy

Cost: $0
Students enrolled: N/A
Total: N/A

9. Graphic Design Bootcamp
Cost: $261
Students enrolled: 73,727
Total: $19,242,747

10. Photography: Complete Guide
Cost: $261
Students enrolled: 123,136
Total: $32,138,496

Disclaimer: The prices of the above courses sometimes differ due to frequent discounts/sales. Therefore, the actual total may be less than the above amounts, but will still generate a healthy profit. After all, it's passive income so even if the course sold for $30 instead of $300, that's still profit for a one time effort. Plus, the lower cost is likely to attract way more sales that might take you back up to the $300 anyway.

As we can see from this list, transferable skills are a hot topic. To excel in the workplace or even start your own company, you need experience in certain fields and to be constantly developing your skills. For example, the web developer bootcamp has almost 500,000 enrollments. The average web developer salary ranges between $49,380 to $93,670. So, it makes sense that if you're on the lower end of the scale you're going to want to boost your knowledge to get that promotion and a higher salary.

Another reason online courses have flourished is because you can do them in your own time. You also don't have to attend college, costing hundreds of thousands of dollars. You can even go through a course on your lunch break at work, meaning you don't have to take unpaid internships just to boost your resume.

So, it makes sense that when you are developing your online course, you focus on the skills that are in demand. It might not be a carbon copy of what's out there, but it pays to stay on top of the most wanted areas. Digital skills such as coding, design and marketing remain a key focus so should be a consideration when putting together your course.

◆ ◆ ◆

5.11 Money Making Apps

Applications are a very broad tool for making passive income. You can either create your own app and sell it in the app store for a profit, or in this case download an app that in itself is a source of income.

There are many apps you can earn money from that require an active effort. For example ones that allow you to complete quizzes or surveys for cash. They are fine for when you have free time (if you use "I don't have time" as an excuse for not getting your finances in order… this is where you are going wrong!) However, there are also apps on the market that can act as a completely passive income stream too.

For example, Honeygain (https://www.honeygain.com) allows

you to use your device as a gateway, by giving your unused GB's to data scientists. The connections are managed and secured by Honeygain, who state that it helps "scientists solve complex data development problems that help create a better future".

Honeygain will pay you up to $300 a month for 100GB, although they ask for a minimum of 1GB per month. If you have a lot of unused data at the end of the month because you only use WiFi, this is one of the easiest possible ways to earn money. You'll also gain $5 for signing up, and for every person you refer to the platform, you'll earn 10% of their earnings too.

That means, you could earn a maximum of $3,965 a year, which includes just one referral who then contributes the maximum GB a month. If you have lots of friends who never use their data and get them all to sign up, you could easily surpass $5,000 a year. As the saying goes: "One man's trash is another man's treasure!"

Another app worth checking out is PhonePaycheck (https://play.google.com/store/apps/details?id=com.neocortix.phonepaycheck&hl=en_GB), who will pay you for using your phone's processor when you aren't using it. The idea is that it allows companies to test their websites for things such as responsiveness and loading times. It's possible to earn $300 a year on Phone Paycheck, and although that's not as much as Honeygain or similar apps, it's still money for doing absolutely nothing!

It's definitely worth researching the latest passive income apps, as new ones are launching all the time. If you can get paid for no effort other than installing an app and sending out a few referrals, it makes sense to go ahead and do it. Remember, the more income streams you have, the more money you will make. Every little helps!

Once you get the hang of different passive income apps, set a minimum goal of $10,000 a year. Given you can also download Wordpress, YouTube and many other passive stream apps onto your phone, there are multiple ways you can achieve this.

Stay clear of survey apps that pay 25 cents for 20 minutes of your time… you could have created a video or blog post and monetized it in that time! The goal is minimum effort for maximum income, especially when it comes to apps.

◆ ◆ ◆

5.12 Buy and sell websites

You've heard of buying and renovating a property to sell it on for a profit, but did you know you can do exactly the same with websites (https://blog.flippa.com/the-beginners-guide-to-flippa-part-1/)?

One such example is Flippa (https://www.flippa.com), which is the website equivalent of a real estate broker. In fact, the whole concept of this website is to buy one and then "flip" it.

When you log onto the website, you can select which category you want to browse including established websites, starter websites as well as sites ranging from lowest to highest in price. This makes it a very flexible tool, even if you don't have a lot of capital to invest in the idea.

Looking at established sites is a safer bet, as these sites are already up and running, receiving visitors and potentially already making a good profit too. These websites originate from people who've put a lot of time, money, effort and not to mention marketing their websites and are looking to sell it. You can then buy such a website, or do the same with your own website and make a profit.

Like all investments, you need to thoroughly research the process before even considering putting a bid on a site. There are countless websites with frankly terrible domain names that have been thrown together in a hurry in the faint hope of making money. These are the equivalent of going fishing but picking up an old boot instead, and should be avoided.

One of the best things to do is to put the domain through SEM Rush to get some basic stats. If the site is fairly new, contains no backlinks and is generally terrible… don't even think about it. However, if the site has a good domain name, plenty of SEO content and links, and is also generating an income - that makes it a much more lucrative prospect. You'll also need to keep in mind these same attributes when looking to sell a website to generate profit.

Most people choose the 'starter' websites, as these can be bid on for as little as $100 and often have no reserve. It does come down to checking the domain name to see if it sounds viable enough to generate a profit from, as well as looking at the existing stats. If the domain name is www.idea4siteorski.com - or some other ridiculous creation (you'll find plenty of these on website bidding sites!), then stay well clear. It has to be something tangible you can actually flip a profit on.

It's also a good idea to avoid new sellers, especially without any feedback to back up previous sales. This is because it's easy to buy traffic and inflate stats, which is another reason you have to double-check all of what is being said on the pitch page, before you even consider putting a bid on a website.

Say you bought a website for $200 and its niche was gaming. In order to sell it for $5,000, you're going to need to put time and money in working on the SEO, in order to increase the domain authority. It's not impossible, but it will take some work. You can of course outsource this work through hiring a freelancer on Upwork. You'll need to consider your marketing strategy including adding plenty of backlinks, as well as the overall design and content of the website.

If you don't have a huge budget to buy and turn around a website (under $2,000) it may mean you build a small profit with each sale. Gradually over time as your knowledge and confidence increase, so will your sales.

5.13 Develop An App

An application that can be downloaded onto a digital device.

The top-grossing app of all time is Tinder, having made over $249,000,000 to date. Similar apps such as Netflix and Huli have raked in millions too. If you are considering passive income streams, it makes sense to consider developing an app of your own.

It's difficult to imagine life without apps as they do everything from telling us our location to how many steps we walked today. We also use apps for gaming, organization and advice, not to mention social media.

To create an app you will need a solid plan (here a step by step guide) as to what it will actually do and who is your target demographic (https://www.entrepreneur.com/article/231145). If you're not a skilled developer, you'll need to hire outside talent to create the app and road test it.

Imagine you have a great idea which will solve one or more problems, for a high number of people. Starting from the beginning, you'll need to do some market research. How does your idea fit with what's already out there? There is little point trying to create an identical model of something that already exists, especially if it's successful. After all, why would you go to an unknown app versus the best selling one everyone has heard of that invented the very thing you are trying to emulate?

There also has to be an actual need for the app you want to create. No audience = no money. It's really that straightforward.

A good place to check is the Apple App store or Google Play. Not only are you looking at what are the top apps, but it can also give you an idea of what you can feasibly charge. There are hundreds of different app categories, so it's a good idea to find where your app would sit among what already exists.

There are people who've been able to retire from making an app, so it can make for a great source of passive income. You can either earn money from charging per download, in-app advertising or having features that users need to pay for to use.

Developing an app will require some up front costs, depending on the complexity of your app. If you don't have the skills to do this yourself, head to Upwork or Fiver and the price would start from around $1,000. It all depends on your idea and what you actually want the app to do.

Some companies create their own apps so that customers can book or order from them. So, apps can work alongside your existing model or be separate entities.

There is also the option of buying an existing app on a website such as Flippa, and then developing it either to release and gain profit from, or put it back on the marketplace. This can be a great way to test the waters as you can research how that app may perform without having to develop the idea from scratch.

No matter how you develop your app or even what it's about - you need to make sure it's good enough for people to download and better still recommend. Otherwise, you'll make no sales and your app will end up costing more than you'll ever make from it. Forget passive income, think… no income!

So, what makes a good app? There are no set rules, but it does need to have a clear purpose. Is it to inform, entertain, organize or even help others? Narrowing down your niche is absolutely key before you approach a developer to make it for you.

Visuals are really important too. If an app is poorly designed, it will instantly turn viewers off. They are unlikely to rate it highly which will result in poor sales. Take a look at how other apps manage their visual communication. The key is not to directly copy but to take ideas on what would actually work. Think clever color use and easy to read typography.

Don't forget a great thumbnail to grab attention as people scroll through the app store. Consulting your developer or a graphic designer at this stage is crucial as that tiny image along with a great description, could make the difference between customers wanting to download your app or not.

The graphics should flow nicely without any blips. You'll also need to factor in updates as well as fixing any bugs. Overall, your app should give people an excellent user experience regardless of what device they are viewing it on. This is just one of the reasons apps are not a get rich quick scheme, they do take prior research to hit the nail on the head.

A great example in the quiz niche is an app called HQ. They use a live presenter to deliver quizzes to an audience of around 100,000 (with many more millions using the app itself). The quiz will give users a chance to earn cash prizes, but the questions are quite difficult. HQ sells lives and power-ups to get through to the next question if you lose all your lives. Similar to in-app purchases on Facebook, adding them to your app can create a huge source of income.

Say you create an app with lives/powers costing $3-$15 depending on the package. If your app has 500,000 users and only 100,000 by the in-app purchase, you would earn between $300,000 and $1,500,000 from the add-ons alone.

Another way to earn money through your app is by selling advertising space. Users can then pay a premium to remove the ads, or continue using the app for free but see the ads. What you can charge depends on how good your idea is, and the number of users.

Say you create a word game and it really takes off, earning you 50,000 daily users within its first year. Users can either pay $3 to buy the game (a maximum profit of $150,000) or use the app for free with ads. Approach some ad agencies and offer a spot in your app for $100 a day to reach your 50,000 users. That would earn you $36,500 from advertising alone. As your users grew, you could then steadily increase that rate.

6. PHYSICAL PASSIVE INCOME

Passive income isn't confined to people making videos on the internet. Take a look around you, and there are literally thousands of potential passive income streams to tap into.

For the most part, physical passive income is about seizing an opportunity. For example, renting out some real estate in an area where there is excellent rental income to be had. Or, selling advertising space on the side of your business.

there are endless physical passive income streams you could start today. Here are some of the most popular to inspire you.

6.1 Real Estate - Long Term Rental

When you think of physical passive income, one of the top commodities that springs to mind is real estate. After all, it's probably the most expensive asset any of us will ever own.

Real estate has and continues to be a goldmine for potential investors, not to mention those looking for a passive income source.

With property, you are looking for that all-important ROI. The average long term rental income in the US is $1,588 a month for an unfurnished home. It goes without saying that New York, Los Angeles and San Francisco have a way bigger earning potential than an unknown town in the middle of Kansas. You should look to make an 8%-10% profit a year, with long term rental. This means if you bought a condo for $350,000, you can make up to $35,000 a year profit.

Add the capital gain of the property (increasing value with time), and you can see why so many people use it as an income stream. Click here for a free guide to investing in real estate (https://www.fool.com/millionacres/real-estate-investing/articles/investing-rental-property-beginners-comprehensive-guide), that I really recommend you check out.

In fact, the average monthly rent for an apartment in New York is $3,514, which would earn the owner $42,168 a year. If this property owner was smart enough to keep investing back into real estate, and bought 9 other similar condos, they would earn $420,168 a year just on *averaged priced* condos.

If you buy a house, it will steadily increase in value over time. The value depends on your neighborhood, how big the house is, not to mention inflation.

Property development is all about finding a diamond in the rough. The incredible thing is even a relatively small investment can dramatically increase then price when you go to re-sell.

Go to auction houses and check out what's out there. The goal is to pay the lowest possible amount for the property, develop it and sell it for the highest price you can get for it.

Finding a great real estate investment goes hand in hand with the right area. Don't even think about buying a condo just because it's cheap, when it's based in the murder capital of your state. Use some common sense! Check out the local rental and resale prices. Know the crime stats and the types of homes and businesses in the area.

Other plusses include property which is nearby schools or local attractions. If it's a home especially, families want somewhere they can settle down in, so give people what they want by choosing a location that's near local education, shops and other amenities.

Before you buy, get the building checked over if these details aren't already available. Whatever you do, never buy blind! A property can have so many things wrong with it. The last thing you'd want to do is buy a house that has extensive structural problems, for example, when you only have a $10,000 budget to fix the entire place up ready for resale or rental.

Never buy straight off the internet without visiting the property first. Bring along an expert or business advisor if needs be. Know what you're getting into beforehand to avoid any nasty surprises.

There are some property auctions in the USA that allow you to "buy blind". Even if the price is low, you have no idea what costs will be involved to bring the property back up to standard, so these should be avoided or at least considered at high risk. There is usually a good reason why a realtor hasn't been able to inspect the property, so heed this as a warning and only invest in properties you have inspected first.

If the property isn't suitable to live in or is outdated, you're going to need to fix this before you can even think about making a profit. Like we said at the start, it's all about finding a diamond in the rough. Work out what your costings are likely to be before you purchase, and always have a contingency fund just in case your renovations run over budget.

People love open plan living, so see if it's possible to knock through some walls, and really create a large open space. You will need to consult a construction firm and get all the proper paperwork for this.

Property is one of the easiest ways to make a highly profitable return from passive income. You can even get a property management company to take care of the tenants or sale for you.

Always set aside money for renovation/redecoration before you buy the property. Set aside some contingency money for if things run over budget.

When selling a home, every room is important. But, it goes without saying that people love a great kitchen for cooking and entertaining. If you can wow people with this when they walk in, you're way more likely to make a quick sale.

Don't overthink the decor. Keep things bright, neutral and simple. Heavy color schemes or clutter everywhere can really put buyers off. White walls and glossy floor tiles can make any property look expensive, so stick to the formula that works.

Once you've sold or rented your property, pile the money back into the next project. Steadily grow your property empire. Continue to make more money each year and provide yourself with even more security.

◆ ◆ ◆

6.2 Real Estate: Short Term Rental (Airbnb)

As I mentioned already before, short term rental was the second stream of passive income I created, and gave me the most returns.

Airbnb allows you to earn money from short term lets (and here is a guide on how to https://learnbnb.com/airbnb-hosting-beginners-guide/). It's similar to how a hotel would make money, only you are letting the property to one person/group at a time. Plus, there isn't the same level of customer service involved, making it much easier to manage. You can develop this scheme under two main categories: Rent to rent and property managing.

In a "Rent to Rent" model, you rent a property long term and you sublet it short term. Take advantage of the residential rental long term price and the short term tourist rental cost. Try to maximize occupancy, in a similar business model to a hotel.

Within the property managing model, you convince the owner of the house to manage their home for them on a short term basis. This means you'll need to take care of managing all aspects of it, in return for earning a commission which can vary between 10% to even 30/40%. The amount depends on the level of services offered, and also your ability in contracting and dealing. This second scheme can be even more profitable than the first one, having no rent to pay or any investment to make. Anyone can start it with absolutely NO CAPITAL!

The highest gains in real estate are probably through a rent to rent scheme. Say you invest $350,000 in renting properties long term, to re-rent short term through Airbnb, Booking.com, Homeaway, Tripadvisor.com etc. The earning potential is double. There are properties that can double or even triple the initial investment. Let's make an average of 2.5x, that way if you invest $350,000 in rental contracts, you can expect to make a gross profit of $875,000 with a net profit of about $450,000 a year!

Say you buy a property, and in the first year you have a capital of $385,000 (the value of the condo + your 10% profits), and the second year you will have $420,000. With the rent to rent scheme, in 2 years you will make $900,000! This is more than double! Plus the more time that passes, the larger the difference gets!

Of course you can start to rent one property at the time, with an initial investment of $1000/$2000 + agency and deposit costs. Consider this scheme to be one of the first potential small investments you could do with the money leverage system (save to invest) I have mentioned previously.

One Airbnb landlord in the UK made £11.8 million ($15,527,124) in just one year alone. This demonstrates how scalable Airbnb really is, especially when it's mostly passive in approach. This was in London, however Airbnb is actually most successful in Bali, where the average income is $40,903 for those who rent through the site. Other cities that have been incredibly successful include Tokyo, Los Angeles, Barcelona, Rome, Melbourne and New York.

If you live near a tourist area and own property (or even rent it!) you are literally sitting on a goldmine with Airbnb. As I have mentioned previously, the money raised can be used as leverage for other income streams. You don't need to do it full time, but even a few days or weeks can generate some impressive income.

Start by renting out an extra room or a portion of your home. Naturally, the more of your home you are able to offer the more attractive this is to vacationers. The point is to just get started, after all, not everyone has the money to buy a home just to rent out. That doesn't mean you are excluded altogether, so work with what you have and slowly build this up.

However you set it up, you can be selective with how often you rent the space out. You can also screen and communicate with potential renters. This weeds out any potential party throwers, or anyone else who fits the stereotypical Airbnb horror story. You can also verify their government ID and hold a quick phone conversation with them for your peace of mind.

Airbnb only takes a 3% fee on your reservation. Let's take this example (https://www.airbnb.com/rooms/22270947?location=Los%20Angeles%2C%20CA%2C%20United%20States&adults=2&check_in=2020-02-01&check_out=2020-02-08&source_impression_id=p3_1575574956_3F-pLLW%2BWoYwuOV4P), which is a whole house in California, priced at $89 per night. The host gives a discount for hiring for 7 nights, so the total cost would be $806, and after Airbnb fees that would leave $782 profit per week. If the same were to be repeated over the course of a year, that host could earn $40,664, before taxes and expenses.

What makes the platform great is that it acts as a middle-man between you and your guest. This doesn't just include the vetting process, but also finding guests in the first place. Similar to how Upwork connects businesses with freelancers. Without the platform, it would be difficult to drum up the same amount of interest in your property. The result equals safer experiences, but also more of them too.

While you absolutely can start small, the goal is to build it up so you can rent an entire property, eventually moving on to rent multiple properties. It goes without saying that to have the best success, you should pick properties that are in a desirable area. For example, near tourist sites or other points of interest.

If you are going on vacation or you work away a lot, Airbnb is great for turning an income on your property while you're not using it. Remember, every bedroom or home you have that doesn't have a paying guest that night is lost income.

In fact, many have described Airbnb as the new way to do real estate. After all, you don't even need to own a property to get started. Any spare bedrooms you have in your home can be the starting point of what is a very lucrative industry.

It makes sense to research how others have become successful, as you'll need a good rating to ensure high occupancy rates. If you have people staying in your home at the same time as you, you'll need to be sociable and have good hosting skills. The more you make your guests feel welcome, the more likely it is you'll receive good feedback and continue to fill the room, generating more money each time.

6.3 Rent Out Your Spare Room

Unlike the last segment on Airbnb, renting out your spare room follows a similar principle however it can be done without 3rd party input. If you have a spare bedroom, attic space or even an outbuilding with living facilities - it's extra income just waiting to be tapped into.

Say you rent out short term your spare bedroom for $900 a

month, that would make you an extra $10,800 a year, minus taxes and expenses. Even if you are just living in a one-bedroom apartment, you could always sleep on the sofa and rent the bedroom out. If you are starting from $0 investment and really need to make some cash, this is a great way to start. After all, if you're able to cut your rental income from your expenditure, you can use this money to save and invest.

If the idea of renting a room out seems daunting, there are websites you can go through to vet any potential tenants. You could even ask any friends or family members if they wanted the room. The main objective here is to generate as much income as possible from your property.

Renting out a room is a really great source of passive income, and by setting up a contract you will have guaranteed money coming in extra month. You could have the money go straight into a savings account, so that you are simultaneously building a rainy day fund.

If you don't have the time or the capital to start a business, this is one of the easiest forms of passive income out there. There are websites such as Airbnb, Booking.com, Homeaway/VRBO and Tripadvisor. In addition, you could always manage someone else's property on the above websites.

Another alternative is to sublet your rental property, which is legal unless your landlord states otherwise (consult your rental agreement if you're unsure). You'll also need to come up with a written agreement with the person/people you sublet to. That way, all bases are covered and you'll earn money without getting into any problems with your landlord.

◆ ◆ ◆

6.4 Rental Of Assets

Do you own anything that could be rented out to give you some passive income? Everything from vehicles, boats and even household items could earn you a tidy income on the side.

For example, say you own a high-pressure washer that can clean driveways or cars. The average cost to rent one is $200. You can pick a professional one up on Amazon (https://www.amazon.com/SIMPSON-Direct-Medium-Professional-Pressure/dp/B07SBLY5YW/ref=sr_1_12?keywords=high+pressure+washer&qid=1574535265&sr=8-12) for around $1,200, meaning you only need to loan it out to 6 customers for it to pay for itself.

Say you marketed your pressure washer to every house in the neighborhood by putting a leaflet through the door, and you set up some ads on Facebook. Even if you only scored 1 customer a week to hire your machine, that would give you $10,400 of income a year. Or, if you could push that to 3 customers a week it would give you $31,200.

In theory, it actually takes about 1 hour to pressure wash a driveway. So, if you were to loan your pressure washer out to just 3 people a day, that would give you a maximum earning potential of $219,000 per year. Use an online booking system and get someone to deliver/pick up your pressure washer to make it even more passive. Buy two machines to serve even more customers, and that would give you a maximum income of $438,000, based on 3 people renting your machine per day.

Did you know there is a site where you can rent your car, similar to Airbnb? The site is called Turo (https://turo.com), and allows users to rent in a location across the US that suits them. A quick search of cars available to rent in LA, found cars costing between $25 and $185 a day to rent.

Turo offers up to $1,000,000 insurance and includes roadside assistance for your peace of mind. Their website states the average user earns $500, and users who list 3 cars earn an average of $3,000 a month.

There are several ways you could get into Turo or similar car rental businesses. You could either list your own car and take public transport instead to get to work. Or, you could list your car up for rent when you are on vacation.

You could also purchase some vehicles specifically to list for rent. This method will require an up front investment, but given there are a wide variety of car models on Turo, it's not limited to flashy expensive Range Rovers.

If you did list the 3 cars and earned the $3,000 a month average, that would give you $36,000 worth of passive income a year. Given Turo organizes the listing and booking as well as the insurance… that's not bad going!

Another type of vehicle to consider renting is motorhomes. America is a huge country, and motorhomes are one of the best ways to explore it, due to the fact it's your transport and accommodation all rolled into one.

Looking at a quote from Motor Home Republic (https://www.motorhomerepublic.com/united-states-rv-rental), specifically a quote for hiring a motorhome in Denver for 2 weeks. The prices range between $483 and $2,161 for those two weeks. That would give the owners from that particular search, a maximum yearly income of $12,558 and $56,186.

In essence, rental of assets can be anything you own that's not currently in use. From personal property to vehicles. If it's not being used right this second, then there is potential to earn money from it. If you have vehicles or equipment sitting in the garage unused for months on end, it's time to turn it into some passive income.

6.5 Advertising

Physical advertising is a great way to earn a passive income. All it takes is you placing an advert from a company on existing assets.

If your home or business is near a busy street with lots of traffic, you're in a prime location to start charging fees for advertising space.

You can also advertise on the side of your vehicle. This method isn't just for buses - in fact anyone can do it. A great website to check out is Carvertise (https://carvertise.com/drivers). They pay between $300 and $1,200 per campaign, which isn't bad for doing absolutely nothing! All you need to do is allow them to display advertising on the side of your car.

If you did 6 different campaigns with them each year, you would earn between $1,800 and $7,200 a year. Once again for the cheap seats at the back…for doing absolutely nothing! Some of the biggest companies in America advertise through this website, so there are some big bucks to be made. Depending on your vehicle, the payments might actually cover the cost of running your car altogether.

If you have land outside your business that's beside a highway, you can place an advertising board or sign there. It requires very little effort and the longer you allow it, the more money you will make.

Outside advertising is popular with law firms, food and drink companies, the entertainment industry and even other local businesses.

◆ ◆ ◆

6.6 Land Flipping

Land flipping is buying a piece of land with the intention of selling it on for profit. There are many ways you can go about this, (and here we give you an "how to" guide link https://thecollegeinvestor.com/17836/benefits-investing-land), from buying a piece of land and holding onto it until it gains value, or by building a development onto it to sell on. Alternatively, you can also sell it to other builders or developers who are looking to construct a new home on your land.

Why is it worth your time? Well, land is limited and the world's population is steadily increasing. This means the price of land will also increase too.

At the time of writing, there are over 1,200,000 plots of land for sale in the US, listed on LandWatch (https://www.landwatch.com/Land_For_Sale). There are 190,000 pieces of land listed at under $35,000, with many listed at just $1 as an auction starting price. So, if you're not a millionaire, you can absolutely still get into land flipping.

Like all forms of investment, you're going to need to do your homework. Points to consider include the location, how many acres and any existing building regulations. For example, not all land will be suitable or have permission for building new houses onto it. So, if that's your primary goal there is little point in rushing into an auction or sale as you won't be able to do it.

It's worth noting that although building real estate is a hugely valuable commodity, it's not the only way land can be used. For example, you could create a visitor park or even grow your own product on the land. That way, you can still turn a profit while you are waiting for the land to increase in value.

If you are looking to build real estate or sell to a developer, it makes sense to buy land that is in a desirable area and close to other communities. Checking real estate prices in the nearby area is a great way to gauge what you might be able to sell the land on for.

Let's take this 10.58 acre lot located in Folkston, GA (https://

www.landwatch.com/Charlton-County-Georgia-Land-for-sale/ pid/331187227) as an example. It's on the market for $39,900. While it's not the biggest plot out there, you do get a lot for your money. In fact, a quick real estate search for Folkston found plots at less than 1 acre for $24,000.

The listing reads like so: "*10.58 Acre mixed use residential, commercial, development property in Folkton, GA 31537. Property has road frontage on US 1 and along the Rail Road on the North side of Folkston in Charlton County, GA. This property could be an ideal location for an Industrial / Commercial Development, but also has residential potential.*"

While that railroad running through it could be a bit of an issue, the listing also states there is real estate or commercial development potential. If you had the money, there is no reason why you wouldn't be able to develop some offices along the railroad, and maybe a couple of houses further away from the tracks.

The biggest plus is its location, as the 301 intersection runs right through Folkston, connecting it with Jacksonville Florida just 42 miles away. In terms of developing your land, you've already got the potential of marketing it to two states. If you built commercial or residential property here, there is already a wide scope of people you could market it to.

That's just an example to get you thinking. You might even spot a piece of land for sale at $100 and renovate it into something else, or sell it to a developer. It's all about finding the right investment, followed by the right market. If you're not planning to develop the land, it could be a bit of a slow burn but is still worth doing as a form of passive income.

❖ ❖ ❖

6.7 Car Parking

There are almost 270 million vehicles in the USA. Do you know what they all have in common? They all need a place to park.

Creating your own parking lot can be an excellent form of passive income, (although it requires a high amount of capital to start) because unlike a fashion trend there is always going to be a need for it. If you live in a congested city, the need is even greater.

With the right permission you could develop a piece of land and turn it into a carpark. Whether you have the funds to build a multi-story car park or even something basic - people will pay you to park there.

If you live in a busy city such as Los Angeles or New York, a parking lot is an absolute no-brainer. Say you have 100 spaces in your parking lot that's open for 16 hours a day. If you were to charge $4 an hour for parking, that would make you $6,400 a day. Or, $44,800 a week. If you were open all year round that would give you potential earnings of $2,329,600.

Sure, you'd need to pay for the construction, plus security and employees. Then there are taxes and other expenses. It's a pretty large investment. But, it just goes to show how a simple parking lot can actually create a life-changing sum of passive income. You could even open multiple parking lots over time and create a whole parking lot empire.

You can also rent your driveway out for people to park during the week. If you live in an area that is notoriously bad for being able to park, you could really cash in. So, even if you don't have the money to turn land into a parking lot, it's still a viable way to earn passive income.

7. PASSIVE INCOME LIFESTYLE

There are so many ways people contribute to others passive income streams through their daily activities. It's about time you got on the bandwagon, especially when there is some serious cash to be made.

Lifestyle can include everything from fitness to travel and even our home life. For example, say somebody wants to learn how to surf. Why not create a surfing tutorial, upload it as a series and sell it as passive income?

A big trend at the minute is wellness. In fact, the wellness industry as a whole is currently worth $4.2 trillion (https://medium.com/manager-mint/the-health-wellness-industry-is-now-worth-4-2-trillion-866bf4703b3c), and is steadily growing year on year. Think about it, people are stressed, they want to get fit, they can't sleep, they might even want a digital detox. All of these avenues can become passive income streams.

In addition, people want to travel more. There are so many ways to make money from the travel industry, from creating vacation rentals to hiring out your home on Airbnb. If you're on the move yourself, you can even house sit to earn money while you travel.

Understanding lifestyle-related passive income, is about moving it away from just work. It's not a company trying to sell you a product in a corporate setting, rather activities to do with our everyday health and lifestyle.

❖ ❖ ❖

7.1 Fitness program

Almost half (39.6%) of the adult population in US is classed as obese, according to NHANES. This is a huge health epidemic that is only set to get worse. Obesity can lead to a range of severe health problems including heart attacks, diabetes and cancer.

It can be a huge struggle to lose weight or even get fit in the first place. That's why fitness programs are incredibly successful. They offer people practical advice that's free from judgment. Best of all, if it's in a downloadable format, it can be accessed at any time in a way that suits the user.

So, what exactly is a fitness program? Take a look at social media and there are hundreds of thousands of people selling their routines or how to guides to budding enthusiasts. It's a great marketing tool because understandable people want to look like what they are seeing on Instagram.

Who hasn't seen someone in the gym take a selfie and think, "wow, I wish I could have their abs!". Whether you are male or female, have no fitness experience or if you are in the gym everyday - there is always room for improvement.

The weight loss industry is worth $70 billion alone in the US. As someone who is looking to make some passive income, it's an excellent industry to consider investing in. An added bonus is that you could genuinely help someone change their life. It's worth noting that to offer weight loss programs you need to be a qualified dietitian.

So, it's best to stick to fitness programs only, unless you're willing to pay for someone's expertise or if you already have the right qualifications.

Start by creating targeted workouts people can follow. You can put them on YouTube and live off the advertising revenue, or creating your own platform and charge for the downloads.

Uscreen (https://www.uscreen.tv/blog/sell-fitness-programs-online) is one of the many platforms where you can sell your fitness content online. They state the average user earns $7,503 per month, which equates to $90,036. Not bad for a few reps in the gym, huh?!

Simply devise a workout plan, chop it into sections and upload it in high audio and visual quality. If needs be, hire a video editor to really make your content pop. You may also need to buy some music (there is always free content online, or in video editing software if the budget doesn't allow for paid music). Don't forget graphics to make your videos look as professional as possible. Even with the initial outlays, it's unlikely you're going to need to spend anywhere near the $7,503 average site users are earning to get started.

There is no end of fitness classes or routines you could film. From yoga and pilates to high energy dance routines. Spinning is also super popular, as it involves people using an exercise bike to complete endurance routines. You could even keep things simple with weights and basic stretches and training. Why not even create a fitness series that walks through everything you need to know about basic gym equipment and how to use it?

The best time to launch a fitness series is unsurprisingly, at the start of January. Most people over-indulge over the holidays, and one of the top New Year's Resolutions is to get fit. You could also launch a beach body series in the summer too.

Don't forget to turn existing clients into ambassadors for your brand either. Who can resist a dramatic weight loss snap, or even someone completely bulking up in the space of just a few months?

You sell your content as a package or as individual episodes, but it's always great to give people a deal if they buy the whole bundle. Let's say you build your social media following for your fitness page and advertise your program through posts and stories. Let's make this extensive giving people a 30 day fitness plan for $300. After all, telling people they get each episode for just

$10 is a great selling point (or, sell them individually for $15). Make it something they can access via an app as well as a physical download.

Spend all summer building up to the release in January, to the point where you have at least 100,000 followers on Instagram (check here how to create the first 20k folks https://www.hopperhq.com/blog/how-to-get-followers-instagram-2019/). Daily posting, lots of hashtags and even giveaways can all help in the run-up.

You've got your $300 program, and you are going to aggressively market it on all your social media platforms as well as Google Ads. You're also going to release blog posts that are SEO rich so that people find your program for the big release.

If you sell just 1 program a day, that will earn you $9,300 a month, or $111,600 a year. But that's just by selling ONE unit a day! Let's make it 10 programs a day (remember, get your clients on board to display the results!), and you'd earn $1,095,000 a year.

Part of your marketing strategy could also be coming up with a brand. Check out The Lean Machines or Results With Lucy for how they have created a personal fitness brand. In fact, go through your Instagram right now and you're probably already following 10+ people who are doing the exact same thing.

You can take things a step further by designing merch which you will sell alongside your program. Wear it in your videos and tell people if they like it, they can follow the link and purchase it to really get the look. You could sell everything from water bottles to clothing and even basic fitness equipment without having to invest too heavily in the initial costs.

Buy in wholesale and sell for a huge profit. For example, branded water bottles will cost you $2 apiece - sell them for $5. Hoodies will cost you $15 - sell them for $45. Be proud of your branding and display it everywhere. Maximize each sale so that with every fitness program you buy, your customers are buying your merch too.

7.2 House Sitting

When people go on vacation they are leaving behind their home for days, weeks or months at a time. If they have tasks that need doing around the house while they are gone (such as watering the plants, sorting the mail etc), or even pets that need looking after, they turn to house sitters.
House sitting does involve some work to carry out these tasks, or you could even create your own house sitting agency and let someone else do the work. Either way, it's not a full-time job and can offer a lucrative return for little effort.

Some people even use house sitting as a way to score a free vacation, as the homeowners often allow you to stay in the property in return for looking after it. By getting paid on top of this, it really is a win-win situation.

According to housesitter.com, most charge between $25 and $45, which isn't bad going for tending to some plants and walking the dog. If you only need a laptop to work, you could effectively be working two jobs at the same time. Going on the average price, that could earn you an additional $1,000 a month.

If you are considering house sitting, it's important to go through an agency so that the whole process has a middle man should anything go wrong. Some of the best examples include:

Trusted House Sitters
www.trustedhousesitters.com
Fee: £66 ($85)

With Trusted House Sitters, you need to buy one of two plans that will either let you become a house sitter, or also list your own properties too.

It has a great map feature allowing you to conveniently see the locations before you start. The website has been running for almost a decade and there are over 2,500 properties looking for a sitter at the time of writing.

Nomador
https://www.nomador.com/
Fee: €65 ($72)

Nomador has the option to list free (albeit with limited functions) or buy a yearly plan. They have a great sliding tool at the top so you can choose how long you want to sit for, therefore maximizing your income. It's unlikely that 2 day sits will be worth your time or effort, so being able to choose longer sits (up to 3 months!) is great for that all-important passive income. It's only available in Europe, but it is ideal if you are already in that part of the World or want to combine it with travel if you're self-employed.

7.3 Create A Self-Help Series

Self-help is big business, and if you have a particular talent or experience that could help others see the light, why not capitalize on it? Or if you do not have that knowledge yet, why not research it? Remember, the more you learn the more you earn? If you read 3 or more books a week you will be very fast in developing a knowledge which will allow you to help others in different fields.

There are so many categories self-help can fall under. From advancing your career, getting over heartbreak, working through addiction or even becoming more confident.

Or, If you don't have any particular skills in either of these fields, why not find a professional who can create a program for you?

As I noted, the wellness industry is worth $4.5 trillion globally, a figure that's increasing year on year. People are suffering from burnout, looking for ways to find inner peace. They are also looking to get fit and get a better night's sleep.

If you are considering creating a self-help series as a source of passive income, the best place to start is to look at the current best selling ones (https://www.amazon.com/Best-Sellers-Books-Self-Help/zgbs/books/4736). Who are they by, how much do they cost and what topics do they cover are the questions to be asking yourself.

"How to win friends and influence people" was released in 1936 by Dale Carnegie, and has sold over 15,000,000 copies. It doesn't take a genius to work out that even selling each copy for $1 would have brought in some serious bucks by now. It's currently on the Amazon store for $15.26 in paperback. Let's average out those 15,000,000 copies by an average of $10 to account for inflation/the different formats the book is available in. That would generate $150,000,000!

So, you might not achieve the same level of success as Dale Carnegie, but that doesn't mean it's not worth your time. If you can create an impressive, helpful book or video series in the self-help niche, there is definitely a growing audience for it.

7.4 Rentable Transport

Take a look at any big destination and you'll likely find rentable scooters, bikes and even segways. There has been an explosion in the rentable transport industry in recent years. With the push for more environmentally friendly alternatives to cars, it's only set to become more prevalent (see a "how to" guide here https://www.wikihow.com/Start-a-Vehicle-Rental-Business).

If you are keen to invest in this market, the key is to pick the right location. If 4 scooter companies already exist on one particular strip, what's going to make yours any different? Likewise, if you try and set up an electric bike company in a town of just 40 people in the middle of the desert, you're unlikely to have much success.

Generally, tourist areas particularly cities and beaches make for the best rentable transport locations. Santa Monica beach in California is famous for this, but so are many other places right across the world. It's constantly growing, and is something social media influencers have been getting on board with too.

The initial investment will involve deciding on a bike, scooter or even electric skateboard. You will need a facility that will allow people to charge as well as pay for it. Many companies use an app for convenience, which will require an up front cost to develop and test.

You'll also need permission/license to operate in a particular area. The larger tourist areas may have a bigger cost, so it's worth shopping around as well as negotiating.

Once you have everything in place, you'll then need to decide how much you are going to charge users per mile. In addition, you'll need a flat fee if the device isn't returned to a certain location which will cover costs in case of theft or damage.

It may take time to recover your initial investment. However, as people are going to be paying to use your rentable for each mile, the money will slowly build back up. Make sure you accompany your rental business with plenty of marketing so people know you're in their city. The bigger the buzz, the bigger the uptake.

If your rentable items really take off, it will become ingrained in the lifestyle of the local people. This has been the case in California, with people regularly seen commuting on scooters and bikes. For many people it's a much more affordable alternative than owning a car or using public transport.

A big uptake means more income. While your rentals may need occasional updates or maintenance, they are on the whole a very passive industry to invest in.

◆ ◆ ◆

7.5 Inventory Hire

Staying within the rental industry, and hiring essential inventory items for your home, vacation or business, is another form of passive income to consider investing in. Inventory hire can cover anything from jet skis in coastal areas, to binoculars at Mount Rushmore. Essentially, anything that can be rented by tourists or residents alike at any given destination.

A great business that is doing things right is Ibiza Rentals (https://www.ibizahire.com/holiday-equipment-hire). If you're not familiar, Ibiza is a Spanish island that attracts 3.2 million tourists a year. It's a popular destination for sun-seeking Brits, as well as partygoers. Pacha Ibiza is one of the most famous clubs in the world.

This is what the company charges to rent certain items (translated in USD):

Mobility Scooter: $138.50
Air Conditioning Unit $110.80

Professional Jiffy Clothes Steamer $110.80
Mini Fridge $55.40
Wheelchair $55.40
Childs Bed $66.48
Travel Cot / Wooden $33.24/$72.02
Play Pen $33.24
Baby Walker $27.70
High Chair $27.70
Nutri Bullet $55.40
Microwave $55.40
Nespresso Machine $55.40
Pushchair $33.24
Car Seat (all ages) $33.24
Booster Seat $22.16
Bed Guard $27.70

If that business manages to rent out every item simultaneously, that would give them an income of $1,113.82 per day, or $7,796.74 per week, or $2,845,810 per year.

See how such a seemingly small list of everyday (but essential) items can actually turn into huge revenue? If the company were to double their stock (as long as the demand supports it of course...), that could give them a maximum potential of $5,691,620 per year... and so on! This is the gross income, so you'll need to deduct products and storage costs. However, it's still an excellent business idea!

Combine your destination rentals with an excellent marketing strategy and it's a complete winner. You could even create old school leaflets at the airport for tourists who are arriving from out of state. Get a website and pack it with SEO, and of course use social media to its full advantage. Do whatever you have to do to let people know you're in town and ready to loan them items for their stay.

You can even target those who have properties in a particular location. After all, not everyone wants to commit to furnishing their vacation home. Or, say they have extra guests coming that weekend and need to hire a cot from you? Nobody is going to buy one just for one night, so renting it's way more sensible. For you, that means even more income because you can accommodate so many needs.

There are no hard and fast rules about what you hire out, but it makes sense to tailor it to the location. If you're by the sea, boats and even inflatables are going to be in demand. If you're in a ski resort, anything that can keep people or their accommodation extra warm is what they will be seeking out.

Always make sure your items comply with safety according to the laws of the country you're in. You will also need to ensure your items if they are lost or stolen. By taking your customer's details in advance, you can issue penalties for lost items or late returns, so you can really cover all bases here.

Why not turn your inventory hire business into a chain? You could set your business up in several locations, with a website or app where people can order the items they need directly. You can also monitor what items are most in demand, so you can maximize sales.

Like we have said many times throughout this book, it's about getting in the mindset of what people want. Say you're in Florida by the beach. You aren't going to need a tent to go camping, but you would definitely hire a powerful AC unit to keep your family cool. Tailor it to exactly what your clients want in a particular location and increase demand even more.

Don't forget holidays and parades in this either. Take the Pasadena Rose Bowl Parade for example. Over 700,000 people attended the 2019 parade, with numbers growing each year. It's a tradition that people line the streets and camp out, coming from all over the world.

Do you know what each of these people need? A tent, sleeping bags, cooking equipment, food, drink, somewhere to wash etc. Why not capitalize on this event and many others like it, and hire or sell the items they might need?

It's about seeing the demand and going for it. Whether it's luxury goods rentals or everyday essentials. Put in the research of the area and what items are in demand. Even if you start small to test the water. Create a system where people can either hire or buy your items, and if applicable include delivery and pick up too for an extra charge.

You've seen the maximum income potential (before tax and expenses) of one company on a small Spanish island. Multiply that by setting up a business in some of the biggest tourist destinations in America, and the sky's the limit.

7.6 Buy A Photo Booth

With the invention of camera phones, you'd be forgiven for thinking photo booths have become obsolete, but that's absolutely not the case. There are two main ways you could buy a photo booth and turn that into passive income.

The first involves traditional photo booths that are used for passport or ID photography. Both of these have strict guidelines including lighting and how to pose. So, no matter how many likes your selfies have it's just not going to cut it. Most passports do not allow any hair to cover the face, and you must remain expressionless too.

Photo booths ensure your photos will pass inspection, by guiding you on how to pose and printing out clear pictures. They also crop exactly the right part of the head and shoulders. Using a photo booth costs around $5 per person. With very little maintenance required, that's a lot of potential passive income. Place in a mall or even your own store to maximize footfall.

The other kind of photo booth involves events including weddings, birthdays, proms, anniversaries etc. Event photo booths involve adding props and pulling silly faces, and then getting a polaroid print out at the end.

They rent out for an average of $500 per event, meaning there is a lot of potential profit to be made. Recently celebrity endorsements of photo booths have boosted their popularity even further.

If you aimed to score 3 events per week, that would earn you $78,000 a year per photo booth. Say you invested the money back into more photo booths and really got your marketing strategy off the ground. If you were able to purchase 3 photo booths and rent them out for 3 days a week at the same price, that would give you $234,000.

Or, if you managed to get each of your 10 photo booths hired across each location every single night, that would give you $1,825,000. So, you could set up a photo booth in New York, Los Angeles, Miami, Houston etc. Or, create a celebrity event company and hire them out to the biggest parties and clubs. You could even get some long-term rental options going for different bars and tourist locations. Get someone else to do the hard yarn and take a commission.

8. PASSIVE INCOME REWARDS

Passive income can also come from how and where you spend your money. Just by saving or spending money with a particular institution, it can generate a healthy interest rate.

It might seem like an "add on bonus", but you should always compare reward schemes before investing or saving. After all, the more you are compensated the more you will earn.

For example, bonds are an investment given to a company or the government to help them fund new projects. In return, you'll be paid interest on the money you have loaned. Bonds are often viewed as a less risky alternative to the stock market, and can be used to diversify a portfolio.

Say you loaned your local city $1,000 toward the cost of a new school. It would have a maturity of 10 years and a 5% coupon rate. As well as getting the $1,000 back in full, you'd receive regular payments of $50. The more you initially invest, the more you'd get back.

Rewards can cover many different savings and investments, so it is yet another way your money can work hard for you while you save it. Even if you open a regular savings account with a high interest rate, it's a great way for your savings to mature while you consider what you want to spend the money on.

Think of rewards as some compensation toward that thinking time. Instead of rushing out and spending all your money, you are keeping it securely saved. At the same time you are earning interest on those savings. If you strike the right deal, it's a win-win for everyone.

8.1 Government Schemes

Did you know you can save and invest with the government (https://www.usa.gov/saving-investing), and be financially compensated in return? Government saving schemes offer much lower risk than the stock market, which is why they are so popular. In addition, your money will go toward building or investing in your local area.

Typically, government schemes are long term investments. They encourage you to save and mature your money, rather than a "get rich quick" scheme. Given that some schemes have a very high interest rate, they are worth considering, especially as you develop your other passive income streams alongside it. One of the most popular government investment schemes is called treasuries.

Treasuries are debts of the US government. So, if you buy any treasury security you're essentially lending money to the government to help pay off that debt. They come in different forms, including treasury bills, treasury notes, treasury bonds, floating rate notes (FRNs) and treasury inflation-protected securities. Collectively, they are known as treasuries.

Investors consider treasury securities one of the safest ways to invest. This is because the government is able to print money and generate tax revenues. In addition, bankers view treasury securities as having zero credit risk. This means it's highly likely you will receive your initial investment and interest on time. After all, the government would be the last entity to become bankrupt, if this is even possible.

The one downside is that treasuries typically offer a low interest rate, compared with other high risk investments. In general, safer investments offer lower returns. That doesn't mean they aren't worth considering, but it's something to keep in mind. Although, for many the lower risk is actually a plus, especially when you are still building your income streams and don't want to risk your capital.

Using the Treasury Direct growth calculator (https://www.treasurydirect.gov/BC/SBCGrw), I entered an initial investment amount of $5,000, with an expected interest rate of 4%, and a periodic investment of $100, with a 10-year involvement. After taxes, the calculator told me my investment would be worth $22,179.14.

You can completely tailor your investment to how much capital you have, as well as how long you're willing to let it mature. So, if you are looking to invest without high risk, treasury securities are definitely worth exploring.

It goes without saying, however, that treasures do take a while to mature, so they are going to be quite far down on your original 16 saving/investing points I mentioned at the start. Remember though, the more income streams you have, the easier it will be to pass and maintain 7 figures in your bank account.

◆ ◆ ◆

8.2 Credit Card Rewards

Before I even begin this section, I will say loud and clear the following: **Any money you spend on a credit card must be paid off in full every month.** As I have already mentioned before, it's better if you never use credit cards **AT ALL!** Just spend what you have on your bank account TODAY and not what you hope you will have tomorrow. Unless of course, you want to go right back to the start and end up in debt and broke again? Although if you want to know, one of the things I started to avoid after going broke was to use credit cards. I strongly recommend using them only when strictly necessary, for instance for renting a car.

Now we've cleared that up, let's look at some of the positives you can get from owning and **spending responsibly** on a credit card, namely the rewards you can receive for doing so.

Credit card rewards are constantly changing, so I am including information that was current at the time of writing. However, make it your mission to constantly check and keep your eye out for the best deals. Just like you would in every aspect of your business and other income streams!

Rewards can be financial, but also give you other perks such as airline miles. While airline miles aren't specifically passive income, it can help off-set the cost of your next flight, which is technically reverse passive income. After all, the more you are able to save on expenses, the more money you can plow into savings accounts or investments.

here are some of the top credit cards due to their rewards, at the time of writing, according to Creditcards.com:

Capital One® Venture® Rewards Credit Card

APR: 17.49% - 24.74% variable
Intro bonus: 50,000 air miles
Annual fee: $95 (waived for 1st year)
Other perks: Earn 2X miles on every purchase, every day.

Blue Cash Everyday® Card from American Express

APR: 14.49% - 25.49% variable
Intro bonus: $150
Annual fee: $0
Perks: Earn a $150 statement credit after you spend $1,000 in purchases on your new Card within the first 3 months. 3% Cash Back at U.S. supermarkets (on up to $6,000 per year in pur-

chases, then 1%).

Chase Sapphire Preferred® Card

APR: 17.49% - 24.49% variable
Intro bonus: 60,000 points ($750 toward travel)
Annual fee: $95
Perks: 2X points on travel and dining at restaurants worldwide & 1 point per dollar spent on all other purchases.

Discover it® Cash Back

APR: 13.49% - 24.49% variable
Intro bonus: Discover will match all the cash back you've earned at the end of your first year, automatically.
Annual fee: $0
Perks: Earn 5% cash back at different places each quarter like gas stations, grocery stores, restaurants, Amazon.com and more up to the quarterly maximum, each time you activate. Rewards can also be used at Amazon checkout.

Summary: If you're yet to discover credit card rewards, you really should get on that! Credit cards offer payment protection on goods or services you buy. However, as I stressed at the start they must always be paid off each month in full.

You can tailor the card to suit your needs, for example traveling or spending. Let's take the Discover it® Cash Back as an example. According to Mental Floss, the average American spends $101 a day, which is $36,865 over the course of a year. So, 5% of that would be $1,843. As Discover will double the interest earned over your first year, that would give you $3,686 - just for spending as you normally would! Who wouldn't say no to an extra 3,600 bucks?

Say you and your spouse combined your bank accounts to use the same card. If you both spent that same American yearly average, that would earn you both $7,372 in interest alone!

Remember, you must pay every single monthly statement off in full. Otherwise the rewards will be pointless as they will be replaced with debt. But, if you are smart about it, there are definitely some hefty passive income to be made with credit card rewards.

◆ ◆ ◆

8.3 Cashback Apps

Both using cashback apps or creating your own could be sources of passive income. We all buy stuff right? But did you know that just by buying your regular items you could be earning a percentage of the sale back?

Cashback apps work in conjunction with various different companies around the world. This includes industries such as retail, technology, travel and restaurants. When you activate the offers, you will earn a small part of your sale back which will be deposited back into your bank account.

Some of the best-known apps include Dosh (https://www.dosh.cash/?_branch_match_id=592078826446898719), Drop (https://www.earnwithdrop.com/?pid=impactradius_int&clickid=yGqVj9XZkxyJR9zwUx0Mo3E

wUkn1PQ3NnxXJwY0&irgwc=1&c=financialpanther) and Rakuten (https://www.rakuten.com). There is also FreeBird (https://www.freebirdrides.com/sms-download/?_branch_match_id=592078826446898719) which gives you points or cash every time you use Uber or Lyft. That's right, every time you need to go somewhere and tap the app to sort your ride…you will get cash back!

People are taking cashback apps to the extreme by blogging about it and offering an affiliate link to the website. These sign-ups sometimes give both you and the user $10 as a referral fee. If your blog already has a decent level of readership, say 1,000,000 users per month and only 10,000 used your code, that would give you $100,000 in referral fees alone.

Also check other avenues that could give you cashback such as your bank or schemes at work.

Although cashback apps are never going to be enough to retire on, they are still going to contribute to your overall passive income. Earning an extra $1000 a year might not seem worth it, but if you did 10 similar passive activities that would be an extra $10,000 a year.

8.4 Couponing

Imagine you are the beginning of your wealth creation process, like many of you most likely are right now. Your income is close to zero, and you need to save anywhere and anyhow you can start creating your money leverage. Couponing is one such way you can do this, and is part of something we talked about right at the start: reverse passive income.

If you've ever seen the show 'Extreme Couponing' you'll know that people take couponing to the extreme. Not only do they end up paying barely $5 for 3 trolleys full of groceries, it can sometimes be the case that the store actually owes them money back.

Couponing is an excellent method of reverse passive income. The idea is by not paying full price on items, you save money. The more money you say, the more money you have. It does take time to spot coupons and cut them out. You'll also need to use the coupons before their expiry date.

Some choose to bulk buy when couponing to save even more money. This might involve buying 100 bottles of mouthwash at once, or 300 cans of soup. For the most part it seems extreme, but there is logic behind the system.

The idea is that by buying in bulk at a heavily discounted price (such as 95%), you will essentially be stocked up for years, if not life on that particular item. By barely spending anything at all on groceries, you can save thousands of dollars every year.

The reality is few of us have the time or inclination to take it to the extremes that some Americans do. But, even a small saving on essential purchases is helping you to save money.

If you are interested in getting into couponing, it's worth devising a strategy. Find out which stores offer the best deals, and which sources have the best coupons. Plan your visit to the store in advance by making a list that centers around these deals. Maximize your savings on each visit and allow your savings to grow.

9. PASSIVE INCOME INVESTING

Once you've mastered personal money management and explored passive income streams, especially after you have accumulated a good capital via money leverage, the next step up is to look at investing.

It's important to graduate from the "school" of financial self-awareness before looking at more advanced forms of revenue. Once again, along the process do not forget to read, study and learn as much as you can on all the different economics subjects.

The stock market for example is not something you can just throw $1,000 on and tomorrow you've made $100,000. The reality is it most likely can take years to see a profitable return on your initial investment. In any case, I would deem this strategy far too risky as it takes highly advanced capabilities and knowledge. This is because you need to fully understand what you're investing in. Plus, like any investment the value can dramatically rise or fall, so you must be prepared for losses as well as gains.

Outside of the stock market, there are many income streams you can invest in which carry much less risk, especially if you do your research. This next section will fully explain how investing works, what are the most popular forms of investment are.

9.1 Buy An Existing Business

Why start a business from scratch (which is a clear example of active income by the way...), when you can buy an existing one as an investor, and let your partner take care of the operational day to day business?

There are tonnes of reasons why businesses go on the market. Sometimes the owners are retiring and don't have anyone to pass the business onto. Others might want a clean break to try something new. Then there are businesses that have run into financial problems and need to be sold before they close down. Or simply, a business is so successful that you want to be a part of it somehow.

I myself, invested in an Italian restaurant chain, Vianello's (vianellos.com), taking it international and opening the first two stores in the Canary Islands. We now have a plan to open in Miami and then all over the US. I also invested into another Italian restaurant chain called "I love Panzerotti" (ilovepanzerotti.com), with 3 restaurants in South Manhattan opened within 8 months, and a big international expansion plan to follow (based on a mix of franchising and directly owned venues). Both businesses are run by my partners, making them purely passive income streams for me.

Buying a business in itself is a bit of a minefield, and that's why like all investments, it's not for those who lack personal money management or business knowledge. If that sounds like you, you'll need to work on this before you even think about taking on another financial commitment. After all, if you can't manage your own finances correctly, how do you expect to do so for an actual business? Or in any case you always be a silent investor, but still you need to have an eye on the business from time to time and have supervising accounting procedures (which you can outsource though).

Just like buying real estate, before buying a business you need to look at the overall model and the current financial situation, and at some marketing aspects such a brand value and potential of the products and services offered. If the business is existing and isn't turning over a very good profit, why is that? You need to ask yourself very clearly if there is anything you can do to change the situation. If the business is located in a bad neighborhood or simply in a low turnout area, for example, do you have the means to move locations? Above all, is it worth it? If it's not, simply buying the business isn't going to change anything.

The same principle could be applied to a number of different scenarios. Say you want to buy a restaurant but the food is terrible - are you going to fire the chef and get a great one? That would make the most sense, because if you plan to keep things as they are, the same problems will just reoccur and it will turn out to be a very costly investment.

Ask to see the books before you buy. If they are not looking healthy, you need to get to the bottom of why that is. You need to be confident you can change the situation before you even consider shaking hands with the current owner. Buying failing businesses or brands can be a great deal, but it takes a lot of skills and knowledge and some foreseeing capabilities to turn things around.

Make sure you actually visit the premises and do throughout research on the clientele, so you know exactly what you are walking into. You should always seek professional advice before purchasing a business. While it might seem like extra hassle, it can save a lot of problems in the long run.

If you realize that the business is instead going great (although this is the best scenario), it might turn out expensive to purchase a share of it. You still can offer though, like I did, to make that specific business international or to open another store/venue somewhere else in the same Country. You could invest money for the opening, and the founder of the company could manage the day to day business personally, or with trusted people. That way you could gain (on average) up to a 49% share of the company.

It is always advisable that whoever runs the business has the majority of shares and who invests only keeps the minority of them. The higher shares the original founder will have, the higher interest will have into running the business in the best way possible. An investment is considered a good investment when it returns (ROI) in less than 2 years. Some great investments of this kind can even return in one year or even less!!

If your investment is sound, it's still going to take some work to keep your customers happy. For the most part, it can remain a passive income as you can hire employees to take care of the day to day running of the business. But, you'll still need to keep a close eye on proceedings to make sure your investment isn't going down the drain.

There are no set rules with regards to what type of business will make the best investment. It does however help immensely if you at least have some background knowledge about the industry, or it's at least you're passionate about.

Once you've had your offer accepted by a business, there will be some initial groundwork involved. Some businesses might already have a very smooth operation that requires very little or no input at all. Others may need steering in the right direction to really start turning a profit. For the most part, this will require some active effort, rather than being completely passive, unless you hire someone to do the job, which would be an excellent choice and would keep the income under the passive category.

You should aim to get the business up and running at full speed as soon as possible. That means dealing with any urgent problems right away, and creating a business model that is perfectly oiled without you having to constantly step in. This is the point at which you can truly start to reap the benefits of your business as a passive income source.

It's equally important not to buy a business and simply forget about it either - even if it's turning over a healthy profit. If you are the owner of the business with other people managing and running it, it's important to check in with them at regular intervals. You want to be kept in the loop about turnover as well as any issues that need resolving. You should also look to invest and improve your business model wherever possible.

To make life easier, use management software which you can control in real time, to monitor your business. Wherever possible, have cameras in every corner of the physical building, in order to check what is happening at any given moment. It's these small touches that give you control but also peace of mind, especially if you are new to running a business.

You can also buy a business with the intention of running it entirely yourself, or with employees depending on how big it is. In that case, it would not be a passive income stream though. Always better to be a Silent investor and invest in successful ventures. The more of your time the business takes up however, the less passive it will be. If you are looking to buy a business for instant passive income, unless you have others that can run it for you, it will be active income. So it's important to think about your strategy beforehand, especially if you are looking to step away from active income or already have a full-time day job.

In order to do this, you'll need a solid business and marketing plan. This includes both physical and digital advertising and different strategies. After all, you can have the best business in the world but if nobody knows about you it's absolutely pointless.

People want to know who you are, where you are and what you can offer them. Those are the 3 fundamentals of any marketing strategy. Buying a business is in fact a great way to break the ice with your customers as you can inform them it's under new management, or even have a grand opening party.

Your business is going to need a website. If it already has one that you are taking over from the previous owner, make sure all the credentials are supplied (that goes for social media pages too).

Take a good look at your business website, and ask the following questions: When was the last time it was updated? Is it easy to navigate? Does it display well on all devices? Is it aesthetically pleasing? Is it in line with our current target audience and branding?

It might seem daunting to answer all of the above, but it's really important your customers get a great first impression from your website. If your website is quite poor, then you'll need to hire a designer to create you a new one (you can always transfer the domain across).

If applicable, you can also add online booking to your website. This in itself is passive income because people can book for your services without having to constantly man the phones or emails. It not only frees up resources, it means you are effectively open 24/7. You will not lose custom just because you're closed. People can still book with you, and even ask you questions if you install a chatbot on your website.

You'll also need to create a social media marketing plan for your business. If you're not familiar with this, you can either teach yourself or hire a professional. Essentially you want to ensure you have daily content going out on Facebook, Instagram and Twitter. What are your best selling products or services that people would respond best to? Work out a strategy and constantly look to improve it. Building organic reach and followers for your business page is key.

You should also look at email marketing, as well as physical advertising such as posters, leaflets, newspaper ads etc. You want people to know about your business so you need to reach as many people as possible.

Once you've taken care of the marketing, your business has a much higher chance of succeeding. Combine this with a great initial investment, and you have every chance of making a successful passive income from buying an existing business.

And last but not least, you need a funnel. A funnel is a combination of online systems and techniques (check clickfunnels.com) to drive your potential customer straight to a purchase/conversion. Every business - no matter how big or small it is - has some kind of sales funnel in place.

It starts with generating leads for your business through marketing or advertising. This creates leads, such as customers clicking on your website, or getting them through the door if you own a physical retail space. Once they are on your website or in your store, this then converts into sales. It's a process, whereby each link of the chain leads to the end result.

Here is a guide on how to buy an existing business (https://www.fundera.com/blog/buying-an-existing-business).

◆ ◆ ◆

9.2 Become A Silent Partner

You've probably heard of becoming a silent partner as a way to generate passive income. There are pros and cons to this, so let's start with the negative points first.

In general, I would not recommend buying an existing business, because in most cases it's too complicated to turn it into a highly profitable one. To clarify, when I say an existing business, I mean a well established company with a good turnover and solid profits. So, do not "directly" buy a company. Buy its successful business model and try to replicate it somewhere else. Create another company together with the founder of that venture, which is doing exactly the same somewhere else. This way the cost of your investment will be much lower (as it is a "duplicate" company you are investing in, with virtually no value).

It's better to find a winning business, and make an offer to the owner to create an international chain. That way you can open more venues, where you could then enter as a silent investor, and be a partner in a new company, which takes care of the international venues' opening. That way, you can let the founder and their team run the day to day operations.

The idea of running an existing business belongs to the active streams of income, so we should stick to our "passive income" plan and just create an additional passive stream which gives us time to develop other streams of passive income and does not drive us back to our 9 to 5 job.

Become a silent partner

The role of a silent partner is limited to putting capital into a business. So, it's more about the pure investment of money rather than the fundamentals of the business model.

The pros of being a silent partner, are that you avoid the stress of also trying to run the business. Inheriting an existing business or even starting from scratch, can take a tremendous amount of work in order to be successful. It's definitely not suited to anyone looking for an exclusively passive input, which is why becoming a silent partner is so ideal.

Silent partners mostly team up with entrepreneurs who need capital to get their business off the ground and/or to expand the business. This may include having them pitch their business to you, showing you the plan of how they are going to get it off the ground, or how they plan to expand, and what the expected turnover is likely to be. You can also look for opportunities to invest in businesses you see potential in.

Like any investment you make, before you become a silent partner you should really do your homework. It's important you feel you can work with everyone else in the business in an effective manner. Although you won't have a hand in running or developing the business, you still want to make sure it's a sound investment and so great communication is key.

Silent partners sometimes come on board within an advisory role too. This makes sense if you have extensive business experience, because the more of this you can share with your investees, the more likely you are to see a healthy return from your initial investment.

The downside of course is that should you dislike the way the business is being run, you are not necessarily going to be able to make changes. You do however have some authority due to your stake in the business.

Becoming a silent partner is all about spotting the right opportunity to invest in. You have to be confident the idea has legs to be able to flourish into a profitable idea. Robert De Niro is a famous example, as he is the silent partner to the restaurant chain Nobu.

Nobu has gained recognition as an upscale worldwide restaurant chain, but that wasn't always the case. Chef Nobu Matsuhisa created the initial restaurant in Los Angeles, after he emigrated from Japan in the 1970s. At the time the restaurant was called Matsuhisa, and it was at this time that actor Robert De Niro started visiting.

It was in 1989 that De Niro saw the opportunity, and made Chef Matsuhisa an offer to open more restaurants by going into business together, with the aim of replicating his existing LA restaurant in New York. However, Chef Matsuhisa's English was still poor, plus he was incredibly busy with his restaurant to even consider opening another. The deal didn't happen at that point, but De Niro continued to drop into the restaurant as he was incredibly fond of the cuisine.

Incredibly, it was a whole four years later that De Niro once again asked Chef Matsuhisa about opening a restaurant called 'Nobu'. This time, De Niro's persistence paid off and the two went into partnership together. Fast forward to the present day, and Nobu has 22 locations around the world, and Chef Matsuhisa has a net worth of $200 million.

9.3 Franchising

Franchising is when a business sells its successful model for others to use. It still remains the same brand, but that particular branch or location is owned either totally or partially by somebody else. You can either buy a franchise (as a franchisee), or create a franchise product for your existing business (franchisor).

If you currently own a business that could work in multiple locations, franchising could be for you. How you earn money is by selling your business model to someone else, and you can also take a cut of the profits too.

Starting a business from scratch can be a lengthy process, which is why franchising is so ideal. It allows you to buy what is already working elsewhere, without having to figure everything out yourself. You can also benefit from advice from the owner about what strategies work well.

Popular models for franchises include fast food restaurants, food trucks, coffee shops, juice bars, bagel stores, sandwich shops and more. It can also extend into other industries such as hair and beauty (blowdry bars or nail salons for example), and general retail stores.

If you are looking to become a franchisee it will require an up front cost. One of the best sites to browse current franchises for sale is franchisedirect.com, who list businesses right around the world starting at just $10,000.

It goes without saying that not all franchises are created equal. There are thousands to choose from, and not all businesses are going to be right for you or the location you intend to put them in.

You'll need to research the company and what you can expect to turn over. Plus, you'll need to know if there are any restrictions on location and what the up front costs are.

One of my companies "I Love Panzerotti" (with 3 venues already opened in South Manhattan and New York City), offers a worldwide franchising scheme. You might want to have a look at the website or drop an email at info@ilovepanzerotti.com for further information about our franchising proposal, and how to open a restaurant of ours according to that scheme.

The great perk about buying a franchise is that once you've got over those initial hurdles, the rest is pretty much done for you. While it's always a good idea to keep on top of any business investment, with others running it for you it's an extremely excellent method of passive income.

You can of course look to sell your current business model as a franchise too (the way I did too for instance). This is a great way to expand your business without having to resort to getting into debt. After all, opening up in new locations costs a lot of money even if your business is doing great. Having someone else stump up the cash means you can earn more passive income with less risk.

Don't just accept the first offer that lands on your door. It's important that the person who buys your franchise knows their stuff when it comes to business. After all, this is your brand and you want to maintain a good company image. You also don't want the business to fail, so vetting potential clients is essential.

Make sure you have a solid business model and a great format (have a look here on "How To" https://www.franchising.com/franchiseguide) before you opt to franchise your business, especially if you have to heavily invest in branding or similar costs. It needs to be something that someone who is completely new to your business can pick up quickly. By providing this information up front, it will ensure the process runs smoothly.

9.4 Vending Machines

Huh, what? Those things in the corner people put a dollar in for some candy? Yep. *"Those things"* are actually potential gold mines just waiting to be tapped into. The vending machine industry in the US is worth $8 billion, so stop sniggering and start listening!

A great example of someone who made their vending machine business work is Reyes The Entrepreneur. In this video (https://www.youtube.com/watch?v=tB5ivEllDsw), entitled "Collecting money from my 4 vending machines", Jaime Ibanez shows how his vending machine business works. His machines take both cash and card, earning him a very tidy profit each month, from what is a super simple idea most of us don't even think about starting.

Jaime follows this same formula again and again in multiple locations. This earns him thousands of dollars in profit a month.

Sure, that's not going to allow him to retire but it shows you what's possible. In one video, he made his initial $80 back 3 times over. Think of that in terms of investing $200 in stock and earning $600 back, and so on. Get even smarter with your locations, products and margins, to turn $200 into $1000. Have the same with 10 other vending machines and that's $10,000 a month, or $120,000 a year.

But, Jaime's passive income doesn't stop there. He uploaded a video about his efforts on YouTube. His channel has almost 30,000,000 views. With Google Adsense also displaying adverts on his video, Jaime earns money every single time someone watches him talk about his passive income. Yes, even just talking about passive income can be classed as yet another passive income stream.

With vending machines you need to start with a great location with lots of foot traffic. Good examples include malls, airports and tourist destinations. If it's in a rough neighborhood, your vending machine could get vandalized, so if possible keep it inside a secure area that gets locked at night.

Speaking of vandalism, and that can be a problem for vending machines, if you don't have the type of safety mentioned above provided by the area which hosts your machines. It's important to avoid the cheap type of containers with no security. The harder it is for people to steal your money or damage your machine, the less repairs/replacements will eat into your profit. Again, stick to secure areas and keep an eye on your machine with security cameras or private security services.

You may also have to pay a small amount of compensation or commission or a rental fee, if you don't own the space you plan to put your vending machines in. You're also going to need some stock. there are so many niches you could cover with this. From health supplements to candy, and even travel accessories for an airport vending machine.

Don't be put off by any of the above. Remember that every passive income stream is going to have its pros and cons. At least if you are aware of this up front, then you can be prepared and plan accordingly.

The initial investment will need to cover the cost of buying vending machines (see if you can get any for free/cheap on eBay, Gumtree, Craigslist etc). Another great website is https://www.usedvending.com/ which sells vending machines, food trucks, food trailers and so much more.

You can also rent vending machines instead of buying them. For example, Vending Solutions (https://www.vendingsolutions.com/vending-machines-sales-and-leasing) offer professional soda or snack machines from $124 a month, whereby you get to keep all the profit. Say the vending machine holds 30 different items, and has space for 8 of each. That would be 240 items it can hold at any one time. Aim to buy each item for $1 or less (go to a wholesaler for the lowest rates), meaning a maximum spend of $240 to fully stock your vending machine. Sell 50% of your stock for $2, and the other 50% for 3 dollars. That would earn you $600, which will give you $236 profit when you include the rental fees.

Those 240 items can easily be sold in 4 or 5 days, if the location is correct. Always test the place where you drop your machines, to maximize your profits as much as possible. Once you've done this, you should expect every vending machine to give you $400 profit every week. This would equal $1,600 month or $19,200 a year. Place 10 vending machines in high profitable locations and you'll have a yearly profit of $192,000. That's more than most people earn from their jobs!

If you place your vending machine in a busy area, you can turn the stock over much faster, even to the point where you refill it twice a week. This all comes down to stocking your vending machine in the right area, with the right products. There's no reason why you couldn't earn $1,500 a month from your vending machine, once you got the formula right. Then it's simply a case of rinse and repeat, adding new locations. Even 2 rented vending machines could bring in $3,000 a month, or $36,000 a year…just from a vending machine!

Vending machines are definitely one to consider adding to your passive income stream. How to start it?? Have a look here (http://www.healthyvending.com/guides/how-to-start-a-vending-machine-business/#ch2). They require the initial investment of buying or renting the machine and stock. But, once they are up and running, the business pretty much takes care of itself, bar restocking, emptying the change and carrying out occasional maintenance.

9.5 Coin-Operated Games

Think arcade games, pool tables and even kids rides at the mall. There are millions of machines like this all over the country, earning money every time someone uses them.

Let's take those grabber machines for example. You know, the ones where you put in a quarter and try and win a stuffed animal? Say it costs you $400 to buy the machine, and $50 to stock it. That $50 will get you 20 stuffed animals at wholesale. The machines are programmed to only let you win every so often, so you already know you're going to be in profit. One lot of stock could actually last months!

Say for every 10 turns, there is one winner of a stuffed animal, and each turn costs 50 cents. That would give you $5 for every $2.50, effectively doubling your profit. Another way of looking at it, is that you're selling every $2.50 stuffed animal for $5. If you program the machine to pick a winner every 20 times, you're selling that $2.50 stuffed animal for $10.

Other items such as pool or air hockey tables require a bit of an up front investment (again, check eBay (https://www.e-bay.com/sch/i.html?_from=R40&_trksid=p2380057.m570.l1313.TR5.TRC2.A0.H0.Xcoin+operated+pool+table.TRS0&_nkw=coin+operated+pool+table&_sacat=0), Craigslist etc). Stick them in an arcade or even a bar or cafe and it's guaranteed earnings, over and over. If your initial investment is $1,000 and you charge $2 a game, you only need 500 games to break even. Who has just one game of pool anyway? The average is about 3 because most people tie. So, that's $6 a time.

Times that $6 by just 5 people who play pool in the bar all day, and that's $35 a day, or $245 a week. Based on those average assumptions, over a year, that one pool table could earn $12,740. Not bad for that initial $1,000 investment! Install 2 pool tables in your bar if there is lots of room, and that's $25,480. The pool tables are literally paying your staff salaries at this point.
Go one further and open a pool hall, and have 10 tables that each brings in $100 a day. That's $1,000 a day (minus any drinks from the bar you'll also set up!), or $365,000 a year if you're open everyday. Hold cash tournaments for your best players and

charge and entry fee, and rake even more money in. Get others to run your pool table or pool hall for you, and keep it completely passive.

It's not strictly a "game" but don't forget coin-operated clothes washing facilities either. The average laundromat can make an average of $500,000 a year gross profit, with a net profit of 35% if run efficiently, according to Entrepreneur (https://www.entrepreneur.com/article/190424). Considering they pretty much run themselves are otherwise run by your customers, that's quite a healthy turnover.

9.6 Private Equity Funds

An alternative investment consisting of capital that is not listed on the stock exchange.

Private Equity involves buying a stake in a company, with the intention of selling those stakes on at a later date for a profit. In order to make a profit, you'll need to sell your initial stake on for more than you initially invested.

There are 3 main routes you can take to get into private equity. Firstly, there is Venture Capital, which are firms that specialize in investing in small private startups. These are typically high risk because it's a new company with no background of how well the product/service is going to do once launched. These companies require what is known as "seed funding" to get their startup off the ground.

It can take a while to see a return on your initial investment, if you do see one at all because of the high risk nature of venture capitalism. However, in the meantime, most venture capitalists look to take a seat on the board to have a say in how the business grows and develops. The goal is to be able to move that startup from a private firm into the public domain, where you'll then be able to cash in on your initial investment.

The second private equity area is to provide growth capital, which is normally provided for existing large firms. The idea is that by bringing in private equity, it will help the company grow. It works out as a cheap option for the firm, plus they will benefit from your expertise. The main goal is to take that large company and expand it further, which will then be reflected in the profits.

One of the most common private equity streams, is called leveraged buyout (LBO). This can involve taking a public firm private, essentially gobbling it up to create a new company. The main advantage of a **leveraged buyout** to the company, is that buying the business is the return on equity. Using a capital structure that has a substantial amount of debt, allows them to increase returns by leveraging the seller's assets. During the process, improvements will be made to the company, and in time the company could even revert back to a public company again. By making improvements and listing it back on the market, you'll then be able to make a profit. It's an advanced form of income, not least because it's a purchase made with debt, using assets from the two companies as collateral.

That just covers the basics of what is a very in-depth and complex topic. It goes without saying that private equity is a very advanced form of passive income, and in some cases does require a substantial active effort especially if you are seated on the board, or in charge of making improvements at the firm.

It is however, something to learn about in your own time to fully understand, as it could become a viable source of passive income when you reach a certain level of wealth. In fact, The Financial Times (https://www.ft.com/content/efee9ee6-8685-11e8-96dd-fa565ec55929) described private equity as: *"the best source of long-term returns for US public pensions, net of any management fees."*

Once you've used your experience to turn your own financial situation around and have developed your own business skills and strategy, you'll be in a much stronger position to understand private equity.

9.7 Crowdfunding

Definition: *Funding a project by raising cash from a large group of people who collectively contribute a small amount to reach the overall goal.*

If private equity, bonds or the stock market feels out of reach, that's not the only way you can get into investing. Crowdfunding is a way of funding your business (**active Crowdfunding**) or venture through donations of money from the public. It is commonly done through crowdfunding websites such as Kick Starter, Indiegogo, Seed Engine, We Funder, Flash Funders and many more.

It is also a great way for you to diversify your investments into different projects (**passive crowdfunding**), cutting down the risk.

How it works is that you post your campaign idea on the platform, with an amount you'd like to raise along with information about it. If people want to support your campaign, they can invest money to help you achieve your goal.

To encourage people to support your campaign, you can offer incentives such as merchandise, acknowledgment or discounts on future purchases on the product you are developing. For example, you could state that for every $20 donated, you will acknowledge that donor on your website.

One of the biggest crowdfunding successes, was the Pebble E-Paper Watch which raised $10,266,845 in just 37 days. At present, 78% of all crowdfunding campaigns reach their funding goal, so it's definitely an avenue to consider.

The beauty of crowdfunding is that it's not a bank loan you have to pay back with heavy interest, plus it doesn't risk existing capital. If your idea is well thought out and you raise the money through crowdfunding, you are set to make an even bigger profit because you won't be factoring in start-up costs.

I've even seen people create campaigns to get into real estate, asking if the other backers would like a share in the profits as their return. This can be done on a low-level scale, especially if you're just starting out. If you have at least $5,000 of capital to invest, there's also a plethora of crowdfunding real estate websites (https://www.fool.com/millionacres/real-estate-investing/crowdfunding/top-real-estate-crowdfunding-sites).

For example, Realty Mogul is currently asking for $5,000 to invest in a new project (https://www.realtymogul.com/investment-opportunity/193744), offering a 7.8% return on your investment. Let's say you did some reverse passive income and side hustles, to the point where you were able to invest $10,000. That would give you $700 extra a year, just from the interest.

On the flip side, you can also use such schemes as the property owner, rather than someone looking to invest. Say you need $300,000 to buy a condo, but you don't have the funds. You could offer a similar deal to Reality Mogul for those looking to invest. The more people who invest, the easier it is to buy the property. With the interest that is made from renting or selling the property on, you'll have enough to pay everyone their share back. Or, you can keep it as a long term solution, that continually gives each investor a small cut.

Others have launched their own companies, products or services. In the entertainment industry, artists use crowdfunding to fund their albums, movies or productions when they don't have the backing of a record label.

For example, say to produce an album it costs $50,000 including studio time, production, distribution etc. If your social media pages had a combined following of 200,000, then you'd theoretically only need each person to contribute 25 cents. Of course in reality, not everyone is going to contribute, but those who do will likely give you much more than 25 cents.

Crowdfunding is helping inventors, entrepreneurs and all-round creators (see here how) realize their ambitions, without having to get into serious debt or financial hardship (https://www.oberlo.com/blog/complete-guide-crowdfunding) . By creating an idea that will form another passive income stream, you can generate some serious capital if you create the right strategy.

Index funds

Pooling money together from multiple investors to buy stocks, bonds or securities.

When it comes to investing in the stock market, most people don't have the time, interest or expertise to pick individual stocks. One of the great features of index funds is that you get broad diversification. This means instead of picking one particular industry or company, your investment covers a wide range of them.

Competitive trends, the management's ability to execute their plans and unpredictable events can cause stocks to rise or fall dramatically. That's why you hear so many people talking about diversifying their portfolio, as it means they are covering all the bases.

If you were to approach the stock market to try and do this with individual stocks, it can be really risky. Even a seasoned financial professional won't always get it right. This is why index funds provide a great solution, as they offer both diversification and minimized costs.

While you can't directly invest in an index (Dow Jones for example), many mutual funds and exchange traded funds (ETFs), track these indexes by holding the same stocks in the same proportion as are in the index.

Index funds can give you broad exposure to the market. In fact, some are so broad that by buying them you will own a tiny piece of almost every public company in America. All that from just one investment!

Index investing can be a useful commodity for both experienced and inexperienced investors. Either way, you will be able to build a well-diversified portfolio.

Index funds are typically low-cost investments compared to buying stocks individually or investing in actively managed funds. You can get access for 0.03% of what you invest, which would equate to $3 a year, if you invested $10,000. This would give you access to over 2,000 stocks.

The lower costs versus traditional stocks, means more money stays within your portfolio. In essence, it's a much simpler and cheaper way to get on the stock market, with a much-reduced risk to your capital.

Both Warren Buffet and Tony Robbins endorse index funds,

especially for those new to the market. Warren Buffet told CNBC (https://www.cnbc.com/2018/06/19/warren-buffett-and-tony-robbins-agree-invest-in-index-funds.html): *"Consistently buy an S&P 500 low-cost index fund. I think it's the thing that makes the most sense practically all of the time."*

Nick Holeman certified financial planner at Betterment, added: *"It's the cheapest and easiest way to diversify your money that you're investing."*

Check out the 12 cheapest index funds to buy (https://www.thebalance.com/cheapest-index-funds-to-buy-4067421) according to The Balance for more information. Essentially, if you are wanting to get on the stock market, invest in some of the world's biggest companies without the huge risk that buying singular stocks can have, index funds are the way to go.

9.8 Peer To Peer Lending

Definition: *Lending money through a middle-man platform in return for a profit.*

Peer to peer lending is built on the idea that you loan someone money in order to generate a return (https://www.financially-independentmom.com/ultimate-guide-p2p-lending). For example, you may lend your money to someone who needs project financing. From the profit they then generate, you can collect interest off the back of it. Eventually, you will also get your money back.

Think of it as a bank lending someone money, only you become that bank. That means you loan the money, collect the interest but also carry the risk. As you might expect, the riskier the investment, the higher the interest rate. That's why peer to peer lending like all forms of investment, requires thorough research before you even think about jumping into it.

The key factors are how much capital is required, how long for and how risky it is. Early repayment of your initial investment can be problematic, as it means less income earned from interest. Likewise, no repayment at all because the investment folded means you could lose your capital.

There are two main peer to peer schemes. One is where you use a peer to peer lending website to invest in multiple borrowers through separate loans. This method allows you to carefully select who you'd like to invest in. However, potential headaches include different interest rates for each loan, different repayment dates, different risk profiles and the hassle of managing all of this.

Alternatively, you can lend to a pool of borrowers with standardized terms attached. For example, you could set the rate at 5% over five years. Companies such as Rate Setter, Zopa and Funding Circle have adapted this very model.

Rate Setter (https://www.ratesetter.com/invest/statistics) for example, states their average interest rate for 2019 is 4.5%, which is comparable with high-yield savings accounts. Say you invested $10,000 over a period of 5 years, you'd earn $4,500 in interest alone. Once you've got your investment back, you'd have $14,500 instead of $10,000, minus any fees or taxes.

Lending Club boasts an average interest rate (https://www.lendingclub.com/investing/peer-to-peer) of 14%. It allows you to invest in consumer credit, appealing to borrowers who need extra cash for home improvements or to consolidate their debt. Each member is vetted, and as you only loan a small fraction to each borrower, this spreads the risk.

A question you want to ask of any P2P lending website, is comparing the average amount borrowed versus how much is returned. Although this still doesn't eliminate all of the risk, knowing that the website vets borrowers and has a good payback rate is a smart idea.

◆ ◆ ◆

9.9 The Movie Industry

According to the Entertainment & Media Outlook by PriceWaterhouseCoopers (PwC), The US media and entertainment industry is set to be worth $825 billion by 2023.

A big part of this comes from the movie industry. Movies can cost anywhere from a few thousand to millions to make, depending on whether it's a budget production or something straight out of Hollywood.

Generating the capital needed to create a film comes from investors. The idea is that money is put forward to gain a lucrative return if the movie is a success. It goes without saying that like any investment, there is an element of risk involved which is why it's an extremely advanced form of passive income.

Plus, investing (click here for the guide https://www.movieinvestor.com/blog/complete-beginners-guide-film-investments) in the movie industry requires a significant amount of wealth to begin with. It's for that reason it's not intended for anyone new to financial management. However, it's still worth featuring because it's definitely an avenue to consider to increase your passive income, once you've mastered the rest of this book and made it well beyond 7 figures.

Firstly, you need to ask yourself if the film has the potential to do well. If it's too niche or has an absolutely terrible plotline, your investment will go down the drain. It goes without saying, it definitely helps to know about the film industry to begin with, or have some great advisors who can talk to you through your potential investment.

For those starting small with unknown films or productions, it will make it financially easier to get into. It can however, be tricky because there might not be a history of the actors or director involved for you to base your investment off. Be wise, ask lots of questions and do your research!

There are also movie crowdfunding websites such as Movie Investor (https://www.movieinvestor.com). These allow for a smaller investment of around $50,000, such as is the case with A Fall From Grace (https://www.movieinvestor.com/movies/15/a-fall-from-grace). Movie Investor also allows you to view the cast and crew, giving you a better idea of whether it has a chance of success or not.

A Fall From Grace for example stars actors from Pulp Fiction and Mulholland Drive - both of which were two of the most successful films ever made. While this is no guarantee that this movie will be as successful, it's still a safer bet than putting $50,000 on a film with a completely unknown audience.

After all, if the cast collectively has legions of fans and a notable social media following, this all helps with the film's promotion. As an investor, it is much easier to get something like this off the ground versus a documentary or film starring people who are new to the industry.

In this case $50,000 is a lot of money, but for the investor who has managed their money well and can afford to part with that kind of money, it could work out pretty well.

Beyond the cinema, there are many ways that movies can make money for years after they are released. Starting with the obvious, and TV subscriptions such as Netflix, Amazon, Sky Movies (and every other TV company in the world) pay for the rights to screen movies.

After this is the hospitality industry such as airlines and hotels. In fact, next time you go on a plane look at the movie list. It's not uncommon to see new releases up against classics from the 1960s. People love variety, and so movies, tv shows and documentaries that are made well have the potential to earn income for years to come.

There are also physical releases which for a while were mostly

DVDs, but is now Blu-ray. Though, check Amazon (https://www.amazon.com/Best-Sellers-Movies-TV-Blu-ray/zgbs/movies-tv/2958935011) and you'll find they still sell both formats, averaging around $15 per item.

Another way movies make money is through merchandising. Take Harry Potter for example, which was first released almost 20 years ago. To this day, new Harry Potter merchandise is being released. There are even Harry Potter shops in different cities around the world, and even studio tours! All of this is generating a whole lot of passive income for J.K Rowling as well as all the investors along the way.

Most independent investors make between 25%-200% on top of their initial investment back. For example, say you were to invest $1,000,000, you would receive between $1,250,000 and $1,500,000 back. In addition, as an investor you own part of the film, so you will continue to benefit from further profits and royalties.

9.10 Cryptocurrency

An electronic form of money that does not use regular currency and doesn't have a central bank. Due to its fluctuating value, there is high risk involved

It goes without saying that cryptocurrency is a bit like the stock market, in that the value can significantly fluctuate. Therefore, you shouldn't put any money on it that can't afford to lose. It's definitely an advanced form of generating revenue although please keep in mind that it is extremely risky, which is why it is included towards the very end of this book.

I personally stay away from the stock exchange and cryptocurrency. However, as it is a valid, although risky, form of investment it's still worth mentioning.

Cryptocurrency was invented in 2008 as a peer-to-peer (Blockchain) electronic cash system. It doesn't have a central bank or government who are responsible for the funds. It is commonly known as "Bitcoin" (the most famous Cryptocurrency).

Between 2009-2010, Bitcoin was virtually worthless. In fact, it took until April 2011 until it reached $1 per Bitcoin. Fast forward to December 2017, where Bitcoin reached its highest value to date, at $19,783. So, if someone had bought 100 Bitcoin back in April 2011, they could have potentially sold it for $1,978,300... not bad for something that was considered "virtually worthless" for the first 2 years following its launch.

At the time of writing, Bitcoin is worth $6,300, so it is definitely on the decline from its 2017 peak. That being said, given we are relying less and less on traditional money, there is always a chance it will creep back up again.

There are many ways you can earn money from Bitcoin. This includes mining, investing, trading, lending, or completing micro jobs in return for Bitcoin.

Bitcoin has and remains a viable source of passive income for the experienced trader. Keeping on top of its worth is essential (https://www.coinbase.com/price/bitcoin). If Bitcoin continues to fall in value, it will offer a good opportunity to invest. As you will be risking your capital, cryptocurrency is an avenue to explore once you have several other forms of constant income so you can withstand any sudden drops in the market.

10. POSSIBLE FUTURE TRENDS

You will notice that many of the existing passive income streams (particularly digital ones) are quite new to the market. With passive income, new income streams are being created all the time, so it pays to do your research so you can keep on the pulse about what's next.

As an entrepreneur, you should also be looking for unique income streams that are yet to be tapped into. There might be key products or services within your business that you can create a passive income stream out of.

An example is gyms who charge members $5 to have their own keyfob as opposed to entering a pin for ease of access. It sounds simple, but with all the processing outsourced it's yet another easy revenue stream - the whole thing can be automated from start to finish. If your gym has 100,000 members across multiple sites, and you only get a 50% uptake for the keyfobs, that will earn you $250,000 of completely passive income. Even the marketing can be done for free on social media or via Mailchimp!

It's about applying the same thought process to your business and existing revenue streams. What simple idea are you missing that could generate a healthy profit with little effort?

Automation may also hold the key to thousands of future passive income streams. As we rely less on physical human effort and have more processes completed by computers, machines or robots - this will pave the way for even lower overheads too. Saas (service as a software) is just one example, which will begin to filter out in other areas of our lives.

Technology is continuing to make things more simple than ever before. We can now order food at just the touch of an app - remember Uber Eats and similar companies are making money from every single sale, even though it's on behalf of other companies. They simply provided the app, and direct the food to the right home all for a commission.

It's key to continue to monitor the industry to keep on top of the latest digital trends. What amazing app could you create, that would have an initial cost that could soon be recouped? Check the app store, check tech websites - get in there with the next big idea before your competitor. Try to anticipate trends.

Always remember that solving people's problems, and doing things better than others, has always been the key to the success of every single business in history. There is still room to create an application which can give better solutions, and improve customers experience or even their life. Never stop thinking about what could change our lives, and look to be the one who provides that solution.

11. SUMMARY

Remember the following earning structure I shared with you at the start? Here's a reminder:

1. Read/learn - BECOME A PERPETUAL LEARNING MACHINE. THE MORE YOU LEARN THE MORE YOU EARN
2. Get your money management and attitude to spending right.
3. Get an initial stream of income (active or passive) with zero investment.
4. Save 25% to invest.
5. Create 2nd income stream (with little or zero investment).
6. Save 25% to invest.
7. Invest to create a 3rd income stream.
8. Save 50% to invest.
9. Invest to create the 4th income stream.
10. Save 50% to invest
11. Invest to create the 5th stream

12. Save 50% to invest
13. Invest to create 6th stream
14. Save 50% to invest
15. Invest to create 7th stream
16. Continuing to save 50%, to invest and to grow income.

Let's break these points down by using the advice and the milestones you have learned in this book, to give you a more tangible path to follow.

- For example, point 1. You have no idea about money management, that's why you're in debt and constantly broke. You're going to fix this by educating yourself daily by reading books, researching other people's stories. You will implement the advice to free yourself from debt (however tough it might be), which takes you nicely into point 2.

- Point 2, which is to understand and apply money management. Those first couple of steps are going to be a huge adjustment, but are vital to be able to move forward with the rest of the steps.

- Point 3: secure an initial stream of income, whether it's active or passive. I really suggest getting a secure, decently paid job (employed or self employed) to cover this point. As I mentioned earlier on, you can't move forward without a regular stream of income. The goal is not to trap you in employment for the rest of your life, rather use it to create leverage later on. If you already have a job, you may want to create a side hustle (active or passive) to generate additional income. You have to work really hard during this stage, but it will all be worth it!

Minimum yearly income target from stream number 1:
Active income: $50,000 to $150,000

- Point 4: Next we come onto saving 25% of your income to invest. This is really steep, and for a reason. Remember, you can implement some reverse passive income to cut down current spending habits to generate this money too. Let's say after tax and any other deductions, you are paid just $2,000 a month. That would mean you need to save $500 a month, which would create savings of $6,000 a year. If that seems impossible, remember what I just said about reverse passive income and side hustles!

- Point 5: You are then going to follow a repeating pattern of saving to invest, and using the savings as leverage to create further income streams. However, as I mentioned many of these can be started for free or very little investment. So, say you still have zero to invest - have a look at all the income ideas I shared with you that you could start for free or very little. As an example, get freelancing on Upwork, become a consultant, write a blog and fill it with paid adverts (affiliate marketing), start a rent business on Airbnb (property management at zero investment) - whatever it is, just get on and do it! Semi - active or fully passive - it doesn't matter, so long as it's a second income stream you're generating.

Minimum yearly income target from stream number 2:
Passive income: $100,000 to $500,000

At this stage, you'll be about a month in. You might still be working to clear your debts and also still educating yourself about money. That's fine, as money management is an ongoing process. Just make sure you are starting to look at growing your income stream. By month two, you should have a minimum of $1,000 saved (from savings and from our example of basic salary, side hustles and reverse passive income streams) and you'll have at least two income streams. It's now time to think about using that money as leverage (while continuing to save as much as you can). Your income will start to grow very soon now.

- Point 6: The same for the amount of money saved to invest.

- Point 7: At this point you can start to diversify such as looking at digital passive income. It's your third stream of income. For example, start a YouTube channel or blog that is monetized. Or, start a Twitch stream, or even create POD (print on demand) products to sell on your new drop shipping store. There may be some small investment required, which is where you can use some of your savings as leverage. This might include creating a drop shipping website, or paying a designer on Upwork to create t-shirt designs for your POD store. Research which method is most likely to work for you, as you'll need your earnings to increase from whatever you choose. Plus, you'll need to get to grips with marketing to really promote your products.

Minimum yearly income target from stream number 3:
Passive income: $200,000

- Point 8: By month 3, aim to have savings through your employment or self employment job, reverse passive income strategies, side hustles, freelancing, consulting and passive income streams. You now have enough income to increase your savings to 50% of what you earn.

- Point 9: You are now going to look at adding another passive income stream (the 4th one), all while continuing your active/passive income streams. Remember, not all income streams are active, actually just one is, so although it sounds a lot of work, many of the methods either require a one time effort, or just a small amount of effort. That is why you should dedicate one entire full month to start one each passive stream, and then it will work for you with no or very small additional work.

For example, it took me about one month to write this book, and (hopefully) it will give me some income for a pretty long time ahead. You could do the same, or even create your own blog, which won't take you very long to put together. Post your content with paid ads running on it (affiliate marketing). You only need to spend a small amount of time writing the post and ensuring adsense/affiliate links etc are enabled! Even your digital marketing can be done in advance through social scheduling.

Minimum yearly income target from stream number 4:
Passive income: $250,000

- Point 10: Continuing to follow the pattern of saving to invest while bringing in active/passive income. Saving being the key word here, as you'll have to be extremely frugal. Even when you earn money through your new income streams, you must save (to invest) as much as is possible. Save every cent of it! Look for the right opportunities, and then use your money to create money as a leverage. The saving strategy is aggressive, but it's going to be really rewarding in the end, and you can't hit 7 figures without it.

By following this pattern till the Point 16, while continually educating yourself and looking for new opportunities to make money, this is how you can truly go from being broke to reaching 7 figures. If you give it all you have to reach your maximum potential, your income should start to look like so:

Minimum yearly income target from stream number 5 to 7: Passive income: $200,000 to $400,000

After you read my story at the start, you probably resonated with how a lot of people feel - that we've failed. Whether it's our careers or relationships or indeed money, it's so easy to beat yourself up. Recognizing failure is one thing, but not acting on it is a whole other entity. The thing to remember is that everyone has peaks and troughs in life. The key is not about failure, but how you bounce back from it to become even stronger than ever before.

Money is a sensitive topic, and how we spend it can actually correlate with our emotions. If you have never been taught how to manage your money properly, then it makes sense you started this journey with very little insight on how to keep and make more of it. I've been there myself, and now I look back, I can't believe how much I wasted on excessive spending that literally left me living off bread and milk for six months.

Things are very different for me now, but only because I got my finances in order which was really tough. Learning self-discipline when it comes to money is one thing, but actually implementing it is another. You have to reach that point where you look at your bank balance in cold hard light and think "enough is enough."

It starts with getting a job - if you don't already have one. If you do and it doesn't pay very well, it's time to get a better one or time to add more and more streams of passive income. If you're self-employed, it's time to up your product and marketing strategy to generate more earnings.

Start to put as much money aside as possible to create a safety net plus money to invest. Implement reverse passive income at the same time to cut your outgoings as much as possible. Cut back on spending, sublet your apartment, get rid of your debt - work through every single financial problem you have until the pendulum starts to swing back the other way into profit.

Once you have that steady stream of income and you have built up your savings, it's time to delve into passive income. The goal is to create a profitable passive income stream, save the profits and invest it into the next income stream. Keep going until you reach those 7 figures, which you absolutely will with hard work and dedication.

It doesn't just end there though. You must always be curious to learn more. Study entrepreneurs, read a new book each week. Subscribe to content and watch the news to monitor the markets. Keep your finger on the pulse of what's happening in the world, especially in the financial sectors. Don't shy away because you think it's for people who are educated, instead become the person who is educated.

Learn from your financial mistakes, grow your capital and stay well away from debt. Only then will you be able to get in a position where you can quit work and enjoy the fruits of your labor. While it does take a lot of time and effort, it is absolutely possible to create an amazing life for yourself from passive income alone.

Think about it, do you really want to spend the rest of your life working in a job you hate, barely able to make ends meet? You're never going to live life to the fullest, and you definitely won't ever experience being a millionaire. Don't be the one who complains because you don't have that lifestyle, go out and create it for yourself.

By taking an aggressive strategy to fix your finances, learning to save and generate passive income, it will be one of the biggest things you can do to change your life. Swapping worrying about money to being able to do exactly what you like with it, all because you got off your ass and made it happen.

Seize this moment and this opportunity to take what you've learned from this book to make that change today. Every single day you should not only expand your learning, you should also take active steps to increase your income. Remember, your 7 income streams need to collectively generate $2,739 a day to become a millionaire in 12 months. If you are doing it over 24 months because you need more time to fix your bad financial situation, that would be $1,369. Either way, work hard, and make it happen. Don't stop until financial freedom is your reality.

12. CONCLUSION

FROM BROKE TO 7 FIGURES IN 12 MONTHS: A STEP BY STEP GUIDE TO THE CREATION OF PASSIVE INCOME STREAMS AND TO FINANCIAL FREEDOM FROM SCRATCH.

As the title itself indicates, the aim of this book is to give you inspiration for a journey which I followed, and that anyone can undertake as well. You do not need to be extraordinarily smart (the average IQ of the Forbes 500 list of the richest men in the world is 120.., an average IQ will do). You just need to want it deep inside yourself, you need to want it and be focused and ready to make some sacrifices to reach your goals for at least 12 months. You have to want this, and educate yourself and make those sacrifices.

There is no other secret. It is not easy, no. I would not like you to get the idea from this book that everything I mentioned can be achieved without "failing" sometimes as well, adjusting and trying again. Otherwise the entire world's population would be wealthy! But it is possible. It is damn possible. Plus, with today's internet technologies it is much much easier than it would have been 30 years ago. Adding streams of passive income sharply increases your possibilities to become wealthy. It is based on statistics and math, and with a mix of self determination. If you focus on both, I guarantee then you will make it. Be resilient, don't give up!

Every stream of income I mentioned above, includes links to online guides and successful case studies that can be used to reach your 7 figures in 12 months. My intention in the future is to write one technical book for every single stream, giving you my own guidelines and instructions on how to make the change to get extraordinary results. So stay tuned for more and follow me on my social media pages and on my website fabbaleinvest.com.

You've almost reached the end of this book now, but it's only the beginning of your financial journey. Firstly, I want to congratulate you on recognizing your situation needs to change. You'll find most people will spend their entire lives with their heads stuck in the sand, even when things are dire. Or, they will bank on becoming famous or winning the lottery to make money. Those my friend - are dreamers. Do you know what a dream is? Pure fantasy.

Becoming financially free is tough, especially if you are in debt or are starting from $0. By reading this book, I hope you've absorbed all the information you need to at least make a start. Your bank balance shouldn't be this alien thing you are scared to check so you never do it - you should be on top of it every single day.

Know what you are buying and how much you are spending. Run your bank account like a business, making sure it's constantly on the up. Once you begin to have both dedication and respect for fixing your financial errors, only then will you be able to progress to saving and investing.

As we talked about, it should be a constant flip between the two. You save to invest, and recoup the earnings to save money. You then further invest, and keep the cycle going. You will build up many streams of passive income that takes care of themselves.

So, if you're sat reading this now with no job, maybe you need to take it back to the start. You need to secure that primary active source of income before anything else. You might even want to look into subletting your apartment so your rent is taken care of and you can save the money instead. Going through those hard early stages is what is going to take you from being broke with no hope of ever breaking free from a cycle of poverty and debt, to having 7 figures in your account.

Educating yourself about money is paramount, but it's also very changing. There is always new information and success stories you need to keep on top of. Look to grow your knowledge every day, meet people, network, discover new strategies and schemes until you make it. Don't jump in with big risks either - get savvy and build your way up gradually, always having a safety net to fall back on.

I call this an "aggressive guide" because that's exactly what it is.

You have to take real action, every single day considering every purchase. You can't just stop at saving at $1,000 either. You have to aggressively save as much money as possible, and constantly save at least 25% of your income, looking to increase this to 50% as soon as possible. Don't forget cutting back on expenses and clearing your debt too! Then, you need to start building as many passive income streams as possible.

From reading this book, I want you to make real change, creating progress every single day. I want you to own up to yourself about where you've been going wrong, and why it's taken you until now to figure you'll never hit 7 figures unless you change.

Remove negative, toxic or unhelpful influences from your life. Curb your emotional spending habits. Work hard every single day at earning, saving, investing and educating yourself.

Only then will you truly be on course to hit 7 figures and maintain it. You can then say goodbye to the 9-5, living in the rat race that so many view as the only way to get by. You want better than that? Then work for it. Use this book as your financial bible and constantly do better, every single day.

Now you've read this book, you know you have what it takes and I can't wait to see you succeed and hear your success stories, so that others can learn from you too.

Fab Bale

www.fabbaleinvest.com

www.ilovepanzerotti.com

www.dr3am1ng.com

www.vianellos.com

www.habytare.com

Contacts:

email: fab@fabbaleinvest.com

13. FAQ

Can I become a millionaire without using passive income?

Yes, of course it's technically possible. But once again it is all about statistics and probabilities. The more income streams you activate, the higher the chances you will reach 7 figures in your bank account.

Although, it's time to face facts - most of us will never earn anything near to what we dream of being paid. You might even be the hardest working employee of your whole company, and you'll still probably be on a fraction of what you need to earn to become a millionaire, and pay all your bills and taxes.

Passive income is about taking back control. You can earn more money even while you're at work - you are in control! It's simply not the case where you have to accept your paycheck from work as the sum total of what you earn. You can create multiple income streams on the side, so you earn from these too. Save up all your money, invest in other projects and start to achieve the wealth you've always dreamed of.

How do I know when to quit my job?

Well, the best scenario is that your regular job keeps you busy 8 hours a day 5 days a week, which is a lot. Say in the moment you realize that using that time to dedicate it to additional streams of passive income, would generate a significantly higher income - around double what you're earning now. That's when you can start to think about quitting. Time is the most precious resource that we might ever have. When it comes to quitting active income altogether, this can only happen when you've perfected your strategy.

You want to get to a stage where if any one of your 7 income streams failed or had a bad month, then the other 6 can take the hit. If you are just working 1 job for example with no other income, how are you going to cope if you get fired or get made redundant?

Just think about this formula. Your income is equal to "money by time". The moment you realize you earn more by using your time to develop the other passive streams, and you have at least 2 other streams that make double your "active stream", well that might be the right time to quit. That day will come with smart work! If you aim to have at least 6 months of your expenses saved in your account as "rainy day money", this will speed up the process, and cover you in case of any unexpected events.

Why aren't more people following this?

It comes down to fear and a lack of understanding, and ultimately mental laziness. Furthermore, they do not teach this at school! We are conditioned from a young age to believe we must go to college and get a job straight after, and that we must work until we retire. It doesn't have to be this way! You are one of the lucky ones who have figured this out, and have taken real steps to achieve it for yourself. Ironically, nobody at school teaches you how to make money!

Don't worry about other people at this stage. You are not responsible for anyone else but yourself, so focus on your financial journey. Going from being broke to financially free is a mammoth task, and for many the effort involved seems too much, even though it could lead to them never having to work again! Be a leader, not a follower and make it happen regardless of if the world tells you otherwise.

How do I fit creating passive income streams around my job?

Remember how we covered the long list of excuses people use? One of which is "I don't have time". I reiterate what I said about every single person having the same amount of hours in the day.

Working 40+ hours a week is tough, and if you take care of a family too your time will be even more stretched. That's still no excuse for not going ahead and doing everything I taught you in this book, in fact, if anything that crazy lifestyle is all the more reason *to do it*.

A good place to start is checking out this article on how 16 entrepreneurs spend their lunch break (https://www.gobankingrates.com/making-money/entrepreneur/how-entrepreneurs-spend-lunch-break). When you find how highly successful people compartmentalize their time, you'll realize the following: there is zero room for procrastination.

That 2 hours in the evening you spend gaming or browsing Facebook? You could have written 4 blog posts or created a YouTube video that would have generated you passive income indefinitely. You could have even spent that time going through your spending this month to work out why you don't have enough left at the end of the month.

Every single aspect comes down to taking responsibility and actually working hard for what you want to achieve out of life. There is zero room for excuses in this!

Passive Income Myths

So I've spent the majority of this book telling you about passive income and how to achieve each stream, including how it works and what to look out for. Now it's time to debunk some of the myths you probably have heard about passive income.

There's No Money In It

Well, not unless you try! I'm guessing you didn't read the part where the top bloggers are pulling in $41,000,000 a month, despite starting from scratch like you and me?

While it's true some forms of passive income aren't worth your time, or take a lot of active effort to make them work... you couldn't be more wrong to assume they don't earn you any money!

Like everything you do in life, finding the right streams of passive income doesn't just take hard work, it also takes strategy. For example, say you want to start a vending machine business but you don't know anything about it and aren't willing to put the time in to learn... it could still work out for you, but the chances are you'll struggle. After all, if you don't know about costings, or which products and locations would work best, how do you expect to turn a profit? That's like showing up to college but not listening, hoping to still graduate.

There is so much free content available in the form of articles, blogs, courses and how-to guides on virtually every single passive income stream there is. If you think there is no money in it, you've simply been doing it wrong!

It takes years to see a return on passive income

Not true! Some passive income streams generate immediate profit. Like it was for me, Airbnb rent to rent is just one such example. Amazon FBA and/or drop shipping can obtain exactly the same results. The main advantage of passive income is that you leverage certain technologies, to have a business started faster than it has ever been possible before. Every digital form of passive income needs no shop to be built, no huge expenses that need covering, and doesn't face many of the barriers that traditional ventures face.

Furthermore, the difference between active and passive income is that you're going to have 7+ income streams all working for you at once. So, even if one stream is a long term scheme (such as a high-yield savings account for example), you'll still have other streams earning you money while you wait.

Remember, even streams that do take longer to mature will still be earning you money so long as your strategy is right. Most of the time, if your passive income stream isn't bringing you a quick enough return, the strategy (or most likely the PLAN) is what is at fault. Keep on growing your knowledge, and research examples from successful cases. Do not forget what really makes a difference today on the internet, and especially in the era of social media, such as SMM, SEO and content marketing. Become a master in those fields and every business will be a successful one.

For example, you have a blog that's not getting any visitors so it's bringing in any advertising/affiliate link revenue. At this point, you'd go through your SEO and implement it throughout your copy, images, video and social media strategy. You'd work on building your following and create an email list. Essentially, you'd go over every single aspect until you built it into a highly successful publication with new content everyday, and 5000+

followers. That's a lot more proactive than just complaining about it! Fix the issues, enjoy the financial rewards that will follow.

What to avoid

While this book has hopefully been instrumental in kick-starting your financial management and passive income streams, it goes without saying that there are some schemes/strategies you are going to want to avoid.

Here are just a few...

Quitting Your Job With No Plan/Security

It sounds obvious, but the aim of passive income is to be able to quit your job in time (or within 12 months if you follow this book), and not right away. In fact, if you have no security (at least 3-4 months salary saved, ideally 6), then you are likely going to struggle.

Like we said at the start, getting on top of your finances is key. Without a source of primary income that's going to be difficult, as your passive income should slowly contribute and then begin to take over.

If in doubt, consult a financial advisor who can give you the next steps. Whatever you do, don't quit your job without a plan or any financial backup, no matter how much you hate it!

Get Rich Quick Schemes

Although this book will help you hit 7 figures in 12 months, it's by no means an overnight thing. Many schemes claim you can make $1,000,000 within a week - but this just isn't true unless you win the lottery.

Passive income is about building your plan. It requires putting time and effort and in some cases investment into plausible schemes that actually work, not fake marketing ploys to make someone else rich. While you absolutely can get rich from following the advice in this book, it's advice given to you to follow over the space of a year.

Starting And Quitting

I get it, it can be tough to financially educate yourself and then create passive income streams while also saving money too. It's a lot to wrap your head around, especially when this is completely new territory and up until this point, you've been broke or heavily in debt.

If you were to start a race and quit halfway through, you wouldn't qualify for a time and you definitely wouldn't get a medal at the end. So, what do you think is going to happen if you do the same with fixing your financial problems?

The biggest thing to avoid is quitting. Unless it's quitting a bad financial habit. What you should never quit however, is working smarter on your streams and savings, to create a better financial outlook.

14. FURTHER READING

Every single day you should look to educate yourself on money and entrepreneurship. This includes reading about passive income to learn about the newest schemes, and how to maximize the income of your current ones. With the amount of apps at our fingertips these days, it's simpler than ever to keep your knowledge topped up.

If you don't build your knowledge, how can you expect to reach your potential? Make it your mission to cram in new information through books, videos, courses, podcasts or even networking events.

here are some of the resources I suggest as your starting point:

◆ ◆ ◆

Books:

The $100 Startup by Chris Guillebeau

Synopsis: *"You can change your job to change your life. You no longer need to work nine-to-five for a big company to pay the mortgage, send your kids to school and afford that yearly holiday. You can quit the rat race and start-up on your own - and you don't need an MBA or a huge investment to do it.*

The $100 Startup is your manual to a new way of living. Learn how to:

· Earn a good living on your own terms and when and where you want
· Achieve that perfect blend of passion and income to make work something you love
· Apply crucial insights from fifty ordinary people who made it work with $100 or less

'Thoughtful, funny and compulsively readable, this guide shows how ordinary people can build solid livings with independence and

purpose, on their own terms' Gretchen Rubin, New York Times bestselling author of The Happiness Project."

Link to buy: https://www.amazon.co.uk/100-Startup-Fire-Your-Better/dp/1447286316

Never Get a Real Job by Scott Gerber

Synopsis: "*Young serial entrepreneur Scott Gerber is not the product of a wealthy family or storied entrepreneurial heritage. Nor is he the outcome of a traditional business school education or a corporate executive turned entrepreneur. Rather, he is a hard-working, self-taught 26-year-old hustler, rainmaker, and bootstrapper who has survived and thrived despite never having held the proverbial "real job. In Never Get a "Real" Job: How to Dump Your Boss, Build a Business, and Not Go Broke, Gerber challenges the social conventions behind the "real" job and empowers young people to take control of their lives and dump their nine-to-fives or their quest to attain them. Drawing upon case studies, experiences, and observations, Scott dissects failures, shares hard-learned lessons, and presents practical, affordable, and systematic action steps to building, managing, and*

marketing a successful business on a shoestring budget. The proven, no-b.s methodology presented in Never Get a "Real" Job teaches unemployed and underemployed Gen-Yers, aspiring small business owners, students, and recent college graduates how to quit 9-to-5s, become their own bosses, and achieve financial independence."

Link to buy: https://www.amazon.co.uk/Never-Get-Real-Job-Business/dp/0470643862

Further passive income reads can be found here: https://www.amazon.com/s?k=passive+income&i=stripbooks-intl-ship&s=review-rank&qid=1575063523&ref=sr_st_review-rank

◆ ◆ ◆

Apps:

Calculator: Yes, the free one already installed on your phone! You don't have to have a college degree in math to be able to add up, as the calculator app will do that for you. The problem is not enough people use it properly. When you're in the grocery store, keep a running tally of everything in your cart using the calculator so you don't overspend (remember what we said at the start about knowing how much you can spend).

Also, you can use it for calculating how much passive income you can earn when research a new stream. You can even use it to work out how much of your active income you need to save, as well as working out the interest rates on your savings. Don't just let it sit there… use it!

Home Budget With Sync: If you need help keeping track of your spending, then this is a great app to try (https://play.google.com/store/apps/details?id=com.anishu.homebudget.full&hl=en_GB). You can keep track of all your bank accounts and expenses, and it will even create reports for the last 6 months so you can see exactly where you are going right/wrong. It can be used across multiple devices, so if you need help getting to grips with your spending, download this app today.

Investing Game: If you're not ready to invest in the stock market and have no idea what you're doing - don't panic. The Investing Game app (https://play.google.com/store/apps/details?id=forex.purple&hl=en_GB) allows you to pretend to put money on real stocks. It's a great app to use while you educate yourself about the stock market and build your passive income streams. That way, when you're fully ready to commit to investing because you can afford to risk the capital, you will have practiced what you're about to preach. This is much less risky than throwing money on the stock market with no clue! In fact, there is zero risk involved with this app because although you're investing in real stocks - it's all pretend.

Financial Times: Keeping up to date with the latest in financial news (https://play.google.com/store/apps/details?id=com.ft.news&hl=en_GB) is one sure way to stay ahead of the game. The Financial Times has been around since 1888, and will tell you everything you need to know in the world of business and economics. This can help you spot great investments, new ideas or just broaden your general knowledge about what is going on across the world's markets.

Oval: Get smarter with your money and learn how to save with Oval (https://play.google.com/store/apps/details?id=com.ovalmoney.oval&hl=en_GB). Every time you make a purchase, Oval will round up the figure and add it to your savings account. For example, say you spent $3.40 in Starbucks (P.S: You learned about financial management at the start, make your own coffee and save $$$$ a year!) anyway...that $3.40 would be rounded to $4, with the 60 cents automatically being transferred to your savings.

So, even if you are completely new to saving Oval essentially takes care of it for you. It goes without saying that you still need to be looking to put away as much money as possible, but Oval is great for starting you off. The best part is without you even realizing, you can build up an impressive amount of savings, just by making your everyday purchases.

Websites

There are countless websites you can access for free to build your knowledge of passive income and financial freedom. You can read websites on your way to work if you commute via public transport, first thing in the morning when you wake up, or even on your lunch break. The main thing is to keep on top of breaking news or the latest trends. here are some of my personal favorites:

https://www.entrepreneur.com/ - The clue is in the name! Here you will find advice from others who have started from scratch just like you and made it happen.

https://www.cnbc.com/make-it/ - Insights into how people just like you turned their financial situation around to make it to 7 figures and beyond. They have a great "money" section covering everything from saving to become debt-free. Be sure to read it everyday!

https://www.forbes.com/#4e3d99a62254 - Focuses on business, leadership and entrepreneurs. Scroll down to the bottom to find a customized website for your country, and keep up to date with the latest market trends.

https://www.businessinsider.com/how-to-make-passive-income-investments-real-estate-2018-8?r=US&IR=T - Business Insider is jam-packed with stories of those who have made passive income work for them. The more stories you read, the more information you will gain. Everyone has a different strategy when it comes to passive income, so constantly feed your knowledge to find what will work best for you.

https://www.thebalance.com/investing-4072978 - The Balance is great at breaking down complex financial schemes into easy to understand language. There are so many great topics on here that will help you master all aspects of saving and investing. Sign up to their mailing list so you'll never miss out on their great advice.

https://wealthygorilla.com/ - If being able to spend big bucks is your goal, check out Wealthy Gorilla. They have profiled hundreds of top entrepreneurs from around the world, chronicling everything from how they started out, to where they are now.

https://www.usa.gov/debt - Remember at the start we told you that in order to be successful, you have to kill your debt? Well, the government has some advice to help. It's painful we know, but unless you are debt-free you'll always have financial problems.

https://www.nerdwallet.com/?trk=nw_gn_4.0 - Full of excellent advice from building your credit rating back up, to how to manage your monthly outgoings. Practically every piece of financial advice you've ever looked for on the internet can be found here.

◆ ◆ ◆

YouTube Channels

The best thing about YouTube is that it is absolutely free. There are thousands of successful entrepreneurs who have shared their stories on the video platform, so if you're not subscribed and aren't actively watching the right content, you're missing out.

Foundr Magazine: https://www.youtube.com/channel/UChpWgrkJY_i7F6wwI_TOnrg

As the name suggests, this channel based on the equally popular website talks to founders of major companies all over the world. It delves into how they started and overcame challenges along the way. The content is really accessible even for those starting at $0, meaning everyone can learn and develop their skills by watching and implementing the advice given.

Casey Neistat: https://www.youtube.com/user/caseyneistat

Casey's motto (which he has tattooed on his arm) is: "Do more". If you don't know the story of Casey, he overcame living in a trailer park with his girlfriend and baby son aged 18, to become a highly successful filmmaker. Everyone told him he was a non-starter and that he would fail. Casey is now worth over $16,000,000, and is one of the most successful YouTubers of all time. His channel is full of inspiring content of how he made it happen, and how he is constantly looking to better his productivity. Spoiler alert: He's not a fan of procrastinating.

TED Talks: https://www.youtube.com/channel/UCAuUUnT6oDeKwE6v1NGQxug

Gain insight from some of the most successful and intellectual people on the planet by watching TED Talks. The channel is heading towards 2 billion views and for good reason. It's a great channel to watch while having dinner or on your lunch break at work. Feed your mind, make it curious and learn from what the speakers have to say.

The Wall Street Journal: https://www.youtube.com/channel/UCK7tptUDHh-RYDsdxO1-5QQ

You don't have to be in the big apple to keep up with the latest in business, finance and current affairs. TWSJ YouTube channel is packed with business news and entrepreneurial advice. It's a great way to stay on top of the latest tech trends, so you can constantly be on the lookout for new ways to expand your revenue growth.

Yes Theory: https://www.youtube.com/channel/UCvK4bOhULCpmLabd2pDMtnA

This channel is a bit left field in that it's not strictly related to being an entrepreneur. What this channel does is create risks to generate returns. It's a way of expanding your mind to get yourself away from your comfort zone to do better than you would have otherwise. For example, their video "Spinning a globe and flying wherever it lands" is on the one hand crazy, but makes for an extremely interesting video that's had over 6 million views. It demonstrates how pushing your ideas can create an amazing response in life, so it is very inspiring.

Nate O'Brien: https://www.youtube.com/channel/UCO3tlaeZ6Z0ZN5frMZI3-uQ

If you want tips to become an entrepreneur or start a side hustle - Nate's your guy. The great thing about this channel is it's super accessible to all, even if you are starting from $0. Nate has excellent videos on how he has streamlined his expenditure to generate returns. He also gets pretty real, especially with videos such as "why it costs more to be poor."

CNBC Make It: https://www.youtube.com/channel/UCH5_L3ytGbBziX0CLuYdQ1Q

I'm a huge fan of this CNBC segment/website, and you'll notice

I've mentioned it a few times throughout this book. That's because it gives an amazing insight into the real everyday lives and struggles of entrepreneurs. It asks them the questions you really want to know, to best understand how to implement the winning strategy into your own life too. The channel is packed with stories from entrepreneurs who have started from nothing to become incredibly successful.

Neil Patel: https://www.youtube.com/user/neilvkpatel

If you are struggling to master affiliate marketing or even SEO - Neil is your guy. He breaks down every topic in basic English so absolutely everyone can grasp it. If you are wanting to maximize your passive income potential, Neil's free content is not to be missed.

Tai Lopez: https://www.youtube.com/user/tailopezofficial

With over 290 million views, Tai educates the internet on all things investments, entrepreneurship and life. In his video entitled "Should you drop out of college?" (https://www.youtube.com/watch?v=5OF6vSAyHLY), Tai rightly points out the education system is floored. He states: "The more you learn, the more you earn!", as he tells his followers he reads a book a day. If you are looking to change your mindset about money, his free content is a great place to start.

www.ingramcontent.com/pod-product-compliance
Lightning Source LLC
Chambersburg PA
CBHW070617220526
45466CB00001B/34